My Studio Neighbors

WILLIAM HAMILTON GIBSON

New York 1898

TABLE OF CONTENTS

A FAMILIAR GUEST

Solitude! Where under trees and sky shall you find it? The more solitary the recluse and the more confirmed and grounded his seclusion, the wider and more familiar becomes the circle of his social environment, until at length, like a very dryad of old, the birds build and sing in his branches and the "wee wild beasties" nest in his pockets. If he fails to be aware of the fact, more's the pity. His desolation is within, not without, in spite of, not because of, his surroundings.

Here in my country studio—not a hermitage, 'tis true, but secluded among trees, some distance isolated from my own home and out of sight of any other—what company! What occasional "tumultuous privacy" is mine! I have frequently been obliged to step out upon the porch and request a modulation of hilarity and a more courteous respect for my hospitality. But this is evidently entirely a matter of point of view, and, judging from the effects of my protests at such times, my assumed superior air of condescension is apparently construed as a huge joke. If the resultant rejoinder of wild volapük and expressive pantomime has any significance, it is plain that I am desired to understand that my exact status is that of a squatter on contested territory.

There are those snickering squirrels, for instance! At this moment two of them are having a rollicking game of tag on the shingled roof—a pandemonium of scrambling, scratching, squealing, and growling—ever and anon clambering down at the eaves to the top of a blind and peeping in at the window to see how I like it.

A woodchuck is perambulating my porch—he was a moment ago—presumably in renewed quest of that favorite pabulum more delectable than rowen clover, the splintered cribbings from the legs of a certain pine bench, which, up to date, he has lowered about three inches—a process in which he has considered average rather than symmetry, or the comfort of the too trusting visitor who happens to be unaware of his carpentry.

The drone of bees and the carol of birds are naturally an incessant accompaniment to my toil—at least, in these spring and summer months. The tall, straight flue of the chimney, like the deep diapason of an organ, is softly murmurous with the flurry of the swifts in their afternoon or vesper flight. There is a robin's nest close by one window, a vireo's nest on a forked dogwood within touch of the porch, and continual reminders of similar snuggeries of indigo-bird, chat, and oriole within close limits, to say nothing of an ants' nest not far off, whose proximity is soon manifest as you sit in the grass—and immediately get up again.

Fancy a wild fox for a daily entertainment! For several days in succession last year I spent a half-hour observing his frisky gambols on the hillside across the dingle below my porch, as he jumped apparently for mice in the sloping rowen-field. How quickly he responded to my slightest interruption of voice or footfall, running to the cover of the alders!

The little red-headed chippy, the most familiar and sociable of our birds, of course pays me his frequent visit, hopping in at the door and picking up I don't know what upon the floor. A barn-swallow occasionally darts in through the open window and out again at the door, as though for very sport, only a few days since skimming beneath my nose, while its wings fairly tipped the pen with which I was writing. The chipmonk has long made himself at home, and his scratching footsteps on my door-sill, or even in my closet, is a not uncommon episode. Now and then through the day I hear a soft pat-pat on the hard-wood floor, at intervals of a few seconds, and realize that my pet toad, which has voluntarily taken up its abode in an old bowl on the closet floor, is taking his afternoon outing, and with his always seemingly inconsistent lightning tongue is picking up his casual flies at three inches sight around the base-board.

A mouse, I see, has heaped a neat little pile of seeds upon the top of the wainscot near by—cherry pits, polygonum, and ragweed seeds, and others, including some small oak-galls, which I find have been abstracted from a box of specimens which I had stored in the closet for safe-keeping. I wonder if it is the same little fellow that built its nest in an old shoe in the same closet last year, and, among other mischief, removed the white grub in a similar lot of specimen galls which I also missed, and subsequently found in the shoe and scattered on the closet floor?

I have mentioned the murmur of the bees, but the incessant buzzing of flies and wasps is an equally prominent sound. Then there is the occasional sortie of the dragon-fly, making his gauzy, skimming circuit about the room, or suggestively bobbing around against wall or ceiling; and that occasional audible episode of the stifled, expiring buzz of a fly, which is too plainly in the toils of Arachne up yonder! For in one corner of my room I boast of a prize dusty "cobweb," as yet spared from the household broom, a gossamer arena of two years' standing, which makes a dense span of a length of about two feet from a clump of dried hydrangea blossoms to the sill of a transom-window, and which, of course, somewhere in its dusty spread, tapers off into a dark tunnel, where lurks the eight-eyed schemer, "o'erlooking all his waving snares around."

Sooner or later, it would seem, every too constant buzzing visitor encroaches on its domain, and is drawn to its silken vortex, and is eventually shed below as a clean dried specimen; for this is an agalena spider, which dispenses with the winding-sheet of the field species—epeira and argiope. Last week a big bumble-bee-like fly paid me a visit and suddenly disappeared. To-day I find him dried and ready for the insect-pin and the cabinet on the window-sill beneath the web, which affords at all times its liberal entomological assortment—Coleoptera, Hymenoptera, Diptera, and Lepidoptera. Many are the rare specimens which I have picked from these charnel remnants of my spider net.

Ah, hark! The talking "robber-fly" (Asilus), with his nasal, twangy buzz! "Waiow! Wha-a-ar are ye?" he seems to say, and with a suggestive onslaught against the window-pane, which betokens his satisfied quest, is out again at the window with a bluebottle-fly in the clutch of his powerful legs, or perhaps impaled on his horny beak.

Solitude! Not here. Amid such continual distraction and entertainment concentration on the immediate task in hand is not always of easy accomplishment.

Last week, after a somewhat distracted morning with some queer beguiling little harlequins on the bittersweet-vine about my porch, of which I have previously written, I had finally settled down to my work, and was engaged in putting the finishing touches upon a long-delayed drawing, when a new visitor claimed my attention—a small hornet, which alights upon the window-sill within half a yard from my face. To be sure, she was no stranger here at my studio—even now there are two of her yonder beneath the spider-nest—and was, moreover, an old friend, whose ways were perfectly familiar to me; but this time the insect engaged my particular attention because it was not alone, being accompanied by a green caterpillar bigger than herself, which she held beneath her body as she travelled along on the window-sill so near my face. "So, so! my little wren-wasp, you have found a satisfactory cranny at last, and have made yourself at home. I have seen you prying about here for a week and wondered where you would take up your abode."

The insect now reaches the edge of the sill, and, taking a fresh grip on her burden, starts off in a bee-line across my drawing-board and towards the open door, and disappears. Wondering what her whimsical destination might be, my eye involuntarily began to wander about the room in quest of nail-holes or other available similar crannies, but without reward, and I had fairly settled back to my work and forgotten the incident, when the same visitor, or another just like her, again appeared, this time clearing the window-sill in her flight, and landing directly upon my drawing-board, across which she sped, half creeping, half in flight, and tugging her green caterpillar as before—longer than herself—which she held beneath her body.

"This time I shall learn your secret," I thought. "Two such challenges as this are not to be ignored." So I concluded this time to observe her progress carefully. In a moment she had reached the right-hand edge of my easel-board, from which she made a short flight, and settled upon a large table in the centre of the room, littered with its characteristic chaos of professional paraphernalia—brushes, paints, dishes, bottles, color-boxes, and cloths—among which she disappeared. It was a hopeless task to disclose her, so I waited patiently to observe the spot from which she would emerge, assuming that this, like the window-sill and my easel, was a mere way-station on her homeward travels. But she failed to appear, while I busied my wits in trying to recall which particular item in the collection had a hole in it. Yes, there was a spool among other odds and ends in a Japanese boat-basket. That must be it! But on examination the paper still covered both ends, and I was again at a loss. What, then, can be the attraction on my table? My wondering curiosity was immediately satisfied, for as I turned back to the board and resumed my work I soon discovered another wasp, with its caterpillar freight, on the drawing-board. After a moment's pause she made a quiet short flight towards the table, and what was my astonishment to observe her alight directly upon the tip of the very brush which I held in my hand, which, I now noted for the first time, had a hole in its end! In another moment she disappeared within the cavity, tugging the caterpillar after her!

My bamboo brushes! I had not thought of them! By mere chance a few years since I happened upon some of these bamboo brushes in a Japanese shop—large, long-handled brushes, with pure white hair nicely stiffened to a tapering point, which was neatly protected with a sheathing cover of bamboo. A number of them were at my elbow, a few inches distant, in a glass of water, and on the table by the vase beyond were a dozen or so in a scattered bundle.

Normally each of these brushes is closed at the end by the natural pith of the bamboo. I now find them all either open or otherwise tampered with, and the surrounding surface of the table littered with tiny balls, apparently of sawdust. I picked up one of the nearest brushes, and upon inverting it and giving it a slight tap, a tiny green worm fell out of the opening. From the next one I managed to shake out seven of the caterpillars, while the third had passed beyond this stage, the aperture having been carefully plugged with a mud cork, which was even now moist. Two or three others were in the same plugged condition, and investigation showed that no single brush had escaped similar tampering to a greater or less extent. One brush had apparently not given entire satisfaction, for the plug had been removed, and the caterpillars, eight or ten in number, were scattered about the opening. But the dissatisfaction probably lay with one of these caterpillars rather than with the maternal wasp, who had apparently failed in the full dose of anæsthetic, for one of her victims which I observed was quite lively, and had probably forced out the soft plug, and in his squirming had ousted his luckless companions.

The caterpillars were all of the same kind, though varying in size, their length being from one-half to three-quarters of an inch. To all appearances they were dead, but more careful observation revealed signs of slight vitality. Recognizing the species as one which I had long known, from its larva to its moth, it was not difficult to understand how my brushes might thus have been expeditiously packed with them. Not far from my studio door is a small thicket of wild rose, which should alone be sufficient to account for all those victimized caterpillars. This species is a regular dependent on the rose, dwelling within its cocoon-like canopy of leaves, which are drawn together with a few silken webs, and in which it is commonly concealed by day. A little persuasion upon either end of its leafy case, however, soon brings the little tenant to view as he wriggles out, backward or forward, as the case may be, and in a twinkling, spider-like, hangs suspended by a web, which never fails him even in the most sudden emergency.

I can readily fancy the tiny hornet making a commotion at one end of this leafy domicile and the next instant catching the evicted caterpillar "on a fly" at the other. Grasping her prey with her legs and jaws, in another moment the wriggling body is passive in her grasp, subdued by the potent anæsthetic of her sting—a hypodermic injection which instantly produces the semblance of death in its insect victim, reducing all the vital functions to the point of dissolution, and then holds them suspended—literally prolongs life, it would sometimes seem, even beyond its normal duration—by a process which I might call ductile equation. This chemical resource is common to all the hornets, whether their victims be grasshoppers, spiders, cicadæ, or caterpillars. In a condition of helpless stupor they are lugged off to the respective dens provided for them, and then, hermetically sealed on storage, are preserved as fresh living food for the young hornet larva, which is left in charge of them, and has a place waiting for them all. The developments within my brush-handles may serve as a commentary on the ways and transformations of the average hornet.

One after another of the little green caterpillars is packed into the bamboo cell, which is about an inch deep, and plugged with mud at the base. From seven to ten of the victims are thus stored, after which the little wasp deposits an egg among them, and seals the doorway with a pellet of mud. The young larva, which soon hatches from this egg, finds itself in a land of plenty, surrounded with living food, and, being born hungry, he loses no time in making a meal from the nearest victim. One after another of the caterpillars is devoured, until his larder, nicely calculated to carry him to his full growth, is exhausted. Thus the first stage is passed. The second stage is entered into within a few hours, and is passed within a silken cocoon, with which the white grub now surrounds itself, and with which, transformed to a pupa, it bides its time for about three weeks, as I now recall, when—third stage—out pops the mud cork, and the perfect wasp appears at the opening of the cell. I have shown sections of one of my brushes in the three stages.

This interesting little hornet is a common summer species, known as the solitary hornet—one of them—Odynerus flavipes. The insect is about a half-inch in length, and to the careless observer might suggest a yellow-jacket, though the yellow is here confined to two triangular spots on the front of the thorax and three bands upon the abdomen.

Like the wren among birds, it is fond of building in holes, and will generally obtain them ready-made if possible. Burroughs has said of the wren that it "will build in anything that has a hole in it, from an old boot to a bombshell." In similar whim our little solitary hornet has been known to favor nail-holes, hollow reeds, straws, the barrels of a pistol, holes in kegs, worm-holes in wood, and spools, to which we may now add bamboo brushes.

Ovid declared and the ancient Greeks believed that hornets were the direct progeny of the snorting war-horse. The phrase "mad as a hornet" has become a proverb. Think, then, of a brush loaded and tipped with this martial spirit of Vespa, this cavorting afflatus, this testy animus! There is more than one pessimistic "goose-quill," of course, "mightier than the sword," which, it occurs to me in my now charitable mood, might have been thus surreptitiously voudooed by the war-like hornet, and the plug never removed.

THE CUCKOOS AND THE OUTWITTED COW BIRD

How has that "blessed bird" and "sweet messenger of spring," the "cuckoo," imposed upon the poetic sensibilities of its native land!

And what is this cuckoo which has thus bewitched all the poets? What is the personality behind that "wandering voice?" What the distinguishing trait which has made this wily attendant on the spring notorious from the times of Aristotle and Pliny? Think of "following the cuckoo," as Logan longed to do, in its "annual visit around the globe," a voluntary witness and accessory to the blighting curse of its vagrant, almost unnatural life! No, my indiscriminate bards; on this occasion we must part company. I cannot "follow" your cuckoo—except with a gun, forsooth—nor welcome your "darling of the spring," even though he were never so captivating as a songster.

The song and the singer are here identical and inseparable, to my prosaic and rational senses; for does not that "blithe new-comer," as Tennyson says, "tell his name to all the hills"—"Cuckoo! Cuckoo!"

The poet of romance is prompted to draw on his imagination for his facts, but the poet of nature must first of all be true, and incidentally as beautiful and good as may be; and a half-truth or a truth with a reservation may be as dangerous as falsehood. The poet who should so paint the velvety beauty of a rattlesnake as to make you long to coddle it would hardly be considered a safe character to be at large. Likewise an ode to the nettle, or to the autumn splendor of the poison-sumac, which ignored its venom would scarcely be a wise botanical guide for indiscriminate circulation among the innocents. Think, then, of a poetic eulogium on a bird of which the observant Gilbert could have written:

"This proceeding of the cuckoo, of dropping its eggs as it were by chance, is such a monstrous outrage on maternal affection, one of the first great dictates of nature, and such a violence on instinct, that had it only been related of a bird in the Brazils or Peru, it would never have merited our belief.... She is hardened against her young ones as though they were not hers.... 'Because God hath deprived her of wisdom, neither hath He imparted to her understanding.'"

America is spared the infliction of this notorious "cuckoo." Its nearest congeners, our yellow-billed and black-billed cuckoos, while suggesting their foreign ally in shape and somewhat in song, have mended their ways, and though it is true they make a bad mess of it, they at least try to build their own nest, and rear their own young with tender solicitude. The nest is usually so sparse and flimsy an affair that you can see through its coarse mesh of sticks from below, the fledglings lying as on a grid-iron or toaster; and it is, moreover, occasionally so much higher in the centre than at the sides that the chicks tumble out of bed and perish. Still, it is a beginning in the right direction.

Yes, it would appear that our American cuckoo is endeavoring to make amends for the sins of its ancestors; but, what is less to its credit, it has apparently found a scapegoat, to which it would ever appear anxious to call our attention, as it stammers forth, in accents of warning, "c, c, cow, cow, cow! cowow, cowow!" It never gets any further than this; but doubtless in due process of vocal evolution we shall yet hear the "bunting," or "black-bird," which is evidently what he is trying to say.

Owing to the onomatopoetic quality of the "kow, kow, kow!" of the bird, it is known in some sections as the "kow-bird," and is thus confounded with the real cow-bird, and gets the credit of her mischief, even as in other parts of the country, under the correct name of "cuckoo," it bears the odium of its foreign relative.

For though we have no disreputable cuckoo, ornithologically speaking, let us not congratulate ourselves too hastily. We have his counterpart in a black sheep of featherdom which vies with his European rival in deeds of cunning and cruelty, and which has not even a song to recommend him— no vocal accomplishment which by the greatest of license could prompt a poet to exclaim,

without having his sanity called in question.

The cow-blackbird, it is true, executes a certain guttural performance with its throat—though apparently emanating from a gastric source—which some ornithologists dignify by the name of "song." But it is safe to affirm that with this vocal resource alone to recommend him he or his kind would scarcely have been known to fame. The bird has yet another lay, however, which has made it notorious. Where is the nest of song-sparrow, or Maryland yellow-throat, or yellow warbler, or chippy, that is safe from the curse of the cow-bird's blighting visit?

And yet how few of us have ever seen the bird to recognize it, unless perchance in the occasional flock clustering about the noses and feet of browsing kine and sheep, or perhaps perched upon their backs, the glossy black plumage of the males glistening with iridescent sheen in the sunshine. "Haow them blackbirds doos love the smell o' thet caow's breath!" said an old dame to me once in my boyhood. "I don't blame um: I like it myself." Whether it was this same authority who was responsible for my own similar early impression I do not know, but I do recall the surprise at my ultimate discovery that it was alone the quest of insects that attracted the birds.

Upon the first arrival of the bird in the spring an attentive ear might detect its discordant voice, or the chuckling note of his mischievous spouse and accomplice, in the great bird medley; but later her crafty instinct would seem to warn her that silence is more to her interest in the pursuit of her wily mission. In June, when so many an ecstatic love-song among the birds has modulated from accents of ardent love to those of glad fruition, when the sonnet to his "mistress's eyebrow" is shortly to give place to the lullaby, then, like the "worm i' the bud," the cow-bird begins her parasitical career. How many thousands are the bird homes which are blasted in her "annual visit?"

Stealthily and silently she pries among the thickets, following up the trail of warbler, sparrow, or thrush like a sleuth-hound. Yonder a tiny yellow-bird with a jet-black cheek flits hither with a wisp of dry grass in her beak, and disappears in the branches of a small tree close to my studio door. Like the shadow of fate the cow-bird suddenly appears, and has doubtless soon ferreted out her cradle.

In a certain grassy bank not far from where I am writing, at the foot of an unsuspecting fern, a song-sparrow has built her nest. It lies in a hollow among the dried leaves and grass, and is so artfully merged with its immediate surroundings that even though you know its precise location it still eludes you. Only yesterday the last finishing-touches were made upon the nest, and this morning, as I might have anticipated from the excess of lisp and twitter of the mother bird, I find the first pretty brown-spotted egg. Surely our cow-bird has missed this secret haunt on her rounds. Be not deceived! Within a half-hour after this egg was laid the sparrow and its mate, returning from a brief absence to view their prize, discover two eggs where they had been responsible for but one. The prowling foe had already discovered their secret; for she, too, is "an attendant on the spring," and had been simply biding her time. The parent birds once out of sight, she had stolen slyly upon the nest, and after a very brief interval as slyly retreated, leaving her questionable compliments, presumably with a self-satisfied chuckle. The intruded egg is so like its fellow as to be hardly distinguishable except in its slightly larger size. It is doubtful whether the sparrow, in particular, owing to this similarity, ever realizes the deception.

Indeed, the event is possibly considered a cause for self-congratulation rather than otherwise—at least, until her eyes are opened by the fateful dénouement of a few weeks later. And thus the American cow-bird outcuckoos the cuckoo as an "attendant on the spring," taking her pick among the nurseries of featherdom, now victimizing the oriole by a brief sojourn in the swinging hammock in the elm, here stopping a moment to leave her charge to the care of an indigo-bird, to-morrow creeping through the grass to the secreted nest of the Maryland yellow-throat, or Wilson's thrush, or chewink. And, unaccountable as it would appear, here we find the same deadly token safely lodged in the dainty cobweb nest of the vireo, a fragile pendent fabric hung in the fork of a slender branch which in itself would barely appear sufficiently strong to sustain the weight of a cow-bird without emptying the nest.

Indeed, the presence of this intruded egg, like that of the European cuckoo in similar fragile nests, has given rise to the popular belief that the bird must resort to exceptional means in these instances. Sir William Jardine, for instance, in an editorial foot-note in one of Gilbert White's pages, remarks:

"It is a curious fact, and one, I believe, not hitherto noticed by naturalists, that the cuckoo deposits its egg in the nests of the titlark, robin, and wagtail by means of its foot. If the bird sat on the nest while the egg was laid, the weight of its body would crush the nest and cause it to be forsaken, and thus one of the ends of Providence would be defeated. I have found the eggs of the cuckoo in the nest of a white-throat, built in so small a hole in a garden wall that it was absolutely impossible for the cuckoo to have got into it."

In the absence of substantiation, this, at best, presumptive evidence is discounted by the well-attested fact that the cuckoo has frequently been shot in the act of carrying a cuckoo's egg in its mouth, and there is on record an authentic account of a cuckoo which was observed through a telescope to lay her egg on a bank, and then take it in her bill and deposit it in the nest of a wagtail.

There is no evidence to warrant a similar resource in our cow-bird, though the inference would often appear irresistible, did we not know that Wilson actually saw the cow-bird in the act of laying in the diminutive nest of a red-eyed vireo, and also in that of the bluebird.

And what is the almost certain doom of the bird-home thus contaminated by the cow-bird?

The egg is always laid betimes, and is usually the first to hatch, the period of incubation being a day or two less than that of the eggs of the foster-parent. And woe be to the fledglings whom fate has associated with a young cow-bird! He is the "early bird that gets the worm." His is the clamoring red mouth which takes the provender of the entire family. It is all "grist into his mill," and everything he eats seems to go to appetite—his bedfellows, if not thus starved to death, being at length crushed by his comparatively ponderous bulk, or ejected from the nest to die. It is a pretty well established fact that the cuckoo of Europe deliberately ousts its companion fledglings—a fact first noted by the famous Dr. Jenner. And Darwin has even asserted that the process of anatomical evolution has especially equipped the young cuckoo for such an accomplishment—a practice in which some accommodating philosophic minds detect the act of "divine beneficence," in that "the young cuckoo is thus insured sufficient food, and that its foster-brothers thus perish before they have acquired much feeling." The following account, written by an eye-witness, bears the stamp of authenticity, and is furthermore re-enforced by a careful and most graphic drawing made on the spot, which I here reproduce, and fully substantiates the previous statement by Dr. Jenner. The scene of the tragedy was the nest of a pipit, or titlark, on the ground beneath a heather-bush. When first discovered it contained two pipit's eggs and the egg of a cuckoo.

"At the next visit, after an interval of forty-eight hours," writes Mrs. Blackburn, "we found the young cuckoo alone in the nest, and both the young pipits lying down the bank, about ten inches from the margin of the nest, but quite lively after being warmed in the hand. They were replaced in the nest beside the cuckoo, which struggled about till it got its back under one of them, when it climbed backward directly up the open side of the nest and pitched the pipit from its back on to the edge. It then stood quite upright on its legs, which were straddled wide apart, with the claws firmly fixed half-way down the inside of the nest, and, stretching its wings apart and backward, it elbowed the pipit fairly over the margin so far that its struggles took it down the bank instead of back into the nest. After this the cuckoo stood a minute or two feeling back with its wings, as if to make sure that the pipit was fairly overboard, and then subsided into the bottom of the nest.

"I replaced the ejected one and went home. On returning the next day, both nestlings were found dead and cold out of the nest.... But what struck me most was this: the cuckoo was perfectly naked, without a vestige of a feather, or even a hint of future feathers; its eyes were not yet opened, and its neck seemed too weak to support the weight of the head. The pipit had well-developed quills on the wings and back, and had bright eyes, partially open, yet they seemed quite helpless under the manipulations of the cuckoo, which looked a much less developed creature. The cuckoo's legs, however, seemed very muscular; and it appeared to feel about with its wings, which were absolutely featherless, as with hands, the spurious wing (unusually large in proportion) looking like a spread-out thumb."

Considering how rarely we see the cow-bird in our walks, her merciless ubiquity is astonishing. It occasionally happens that almost every nest I meet in a day's walk will show the ominous speckled egg. In a single stroll in the country I have removed eight of these foreboding tokens of misery. Only last summer I discovered the nest of a wood-sparrow in a hazel-bush, my attention being attracted thither by the parent bird bearing food in her beak. I found the nest occupied, appropriated, monopolized, by a cow-bird fledgling—a great, fat, clamoring lubber, completely filling the cavity of the nest, the one diminutive, puny remnant of the sparrow's offspring being jammed against the side of the nest, and a skeleton of a previous victim hanging among the branches below, with doubtless others lost in the grass somewhere in the near neighborhood, where they had been removed by the bereaved mother. The ravenous young parasite, though not half grown, was yet bigger by nearly double than the foster-mother. What a monster this! The "Black Douglass" of the bird home; a blot on Nature's page!

As in previous instances, observing that the interloper had a voice fully capable of making his wants known, I gave the comfortable little beast ample room to spread himself on the ground, and let the lone little starveling survivor of the rightful brood have his cot all to himself.

And yet, as I left the spot, I confess to a certain misgiving, as the pleading chirrup of the ousted fledgling followed me faintly and more faintly up the hill, recalling, too, the many previous similar acts of mine—and one in particular, when I had slaughtered in cold blood two of these irresponsibles found in a single nest. But sober second thought evoked a more philosophic and conscientious mood, the outcome of which leading, as always, to a semi-conviction that the complex question of reconciliation of duty and humanity in the premises was not thus easily disposed of, considering, as I was bound to do, the equal innocence of the chicks, both of which had been placed in the nest in obedience to a natural law, which in the case of the cow-bird was none the less a divine institution because I failed to understand it. Such is the inevitable, somewhat penitent conclusion which I always arrive at on the cow-bird question; and yet my next cow-bird fledgling will doubtless follow the fate of all its predecessors, the reminiscent qualms of conscience finding a ready philosophy equal to the emergency; for if, indeed, this parasite of the bird home be a factor in the divine plan of Nature's equilibrium, looking towards the survival of the fittest and the regulation of the sparrow and small-bird population, which we must admit, how am I to know but that this righteous impulse of the human animal is not equally a divine, as it is certainly a natural institution looking to the limitations of the cow-bird? One June morning, a year or two ago, I heard a loud squeaking, as of a young bird in the grass near my door, and, on approaching, discovered the spectacle of a cow-bird, almost full-fledged, being fed by its foster-mother, a chippy not more than half its size, and which was obliged to stand on tiptoe to cram the gullet of the parasite. The victims of the cow-bird are usually, as in this instance, birds of much smaller size, the fly-catchers, the sparrows, warblers, and vireos, though she occasionally imposes on larger species, such as the orioles and the thrushes. The following are among its most frequent dupes, given somewhat in the order of the bird's apparent choice: song-sparrow, field-sparrow, yellow warbler, chipping-sparrow, other sparrows, Maryland yellow-throat, yellow-breasted chat, vireos, worm-eating warbler, indigo-bird, least-flycatcher, bluebird, Acadian flycatcher, Canada flycatcher, oven-bird, king-bird, cat-bird, phœbe, Wilson's thrush, chewink, and wood-thrush.

But one egg is usually deposited in a single nest; the presence of two eggs probably indicates, as in the case of the European cuckoo, the visits of two cow-birds rather than a second visit from the same individual—the presence of two cow-bird chicks of equal size being rather a proof of this than otherwise, in that kind Nature would seem to have accommodated the bird with an exceptional physiological resource, which matures its eggs at intervals of three or more days, as against the daily oviposition of its dupes, thus giving it plenty of time to make its search and take its pick among the bird-homes. Whether the process of evolution has similarly equipped our cow-bird I am not aware; but the vicious habits of the two birds are so identical that the same accommodating functional conditions might reasonably be expected. It is, indeed, an interesting fact well known to ornithologists that our own American cuckoos, both the yellow-billed and black-billed, although rudimentary nest-builders, still retain the same exceptional interval in their egg-laying as do their foreign namesake. The eggs are laid from four days to a week apart, instead of daily, as with most birds, their period of perilous nidification on that haphazard apology of a nest being thus possibly prolonged to six weeks. Thus we find, in consequence, the anomalous spectacle of the egg and full-grown chick, and perhaps one or two fledglings of intermediate stages of growth, scattered about at once, helter-skelter, in the same nest. Only two years ago I discovered such a nest not a hundred feet from my house, containing one chick about two days old, another almost full-fledged, while a fresh-broken egg lay upon the ground beneath. Such a household condition would seem rather demoralizing to the cares of incubation, and doubtless the addled or ousted egg is a frequent episode in our cuckoo's experience.

It is an interesting question which the contrast of the American and European cuckoo thus presents. Is the American species a degenerate or a progressive nest-builder? Has she advanced in process of evolution from a parasitical progenitor building no nest, or is the bird gradually retrograding to the evil ways of her notorious namesake?

The evidence of this generic physiological peculiarity in the intervals of oviposition, taken in consideration with the fact of the rudimentary nest, would seem to indicate the retention of a now useless physiological function, and that the bird is thus a reformer who has repudiated the example of her ancestors, and has henceforth determined to look after her own babes.

With the original presumed object of this remarkable prolonged interval in egg-laying now removed, the period will doubtless be reduced through gradual evolution to accommodate itself to the newly adopted conditions. The week's interval, taken in connection with the makeshift nest or platform of sticks, is now a disastrous element in the life of the bird. Such of the cuckoos, therefore, as build the more perfect nests, or lay at shortest intervals, will have a distinct advantage over their less provident fellows, and the law of heredity will thus insure the continual survival of the fittest.

The cuckoo is not alone among British birds in its intrusion on other nests. Many other species are occasionally addicted to the same practice, though such acts are apparently accidental rather than deliberate, so far as parasitical intent is concerned. The lapse is especially noticeable among such birds as build in hollow trees and boxes, as the woodpeckers and wagtails. Thus the English starling will occasionally impose upon and dispossess the green woodpecker. In the process of nature in such cases the stronger of the two birds would retain the nest, and thus assume the duties of foster-parent. Starting from this reasonable premise concerning the prehistoric cuckoo, it is not difficult to see how natural selection, working through ages of evolution by heredity, might have developed the habitual resignation of the evicted bird, perhaps to the ultimate entire abandonment of the function of incubation. Inasmuch as "we have no experience in the creation of worlds," we can only presume.

Indeed, the similarities and contrasts afforded by a comparison of the habits of all these birds—European cuckoo, American cuckoo, and cow-bird—afford an interesting theme for the student of evolution. What is to be the ultimate outcome of it all? for the murderous cuckoo must be considered merely as an innocent factor in the great scheme of Nature's equilibrium, in which the devourer and the parasite would seem to play the all-important parts, the present example being especially emphasized because of its conspicuousness and its violence to purely human sentiment. The parasite would often seem to hold the balance of power.

Jonathan Swift's epitome of the subject, if not specifically true, is at least correct in its general application:

"A flea
Has smaller fleas that on him prey;
And these have smaller still to bite 'em;
And so proceed ad infinitum."

Even the tiny egg of a butterfly has its ichneumon parasite, a microscopic wasp, which lays its own egg within the larger one, which ultimately hatches a wasp instead of the baby caterpillar.

But who ever heard of anything but good luck falling to the lot of cow-bird or cuckoo, except as its blighting course is occasionally arrested by the outraged human? They always find a feathered nest.

In this connection it is interesting to note certain developments in bird life upon the lines of which evolution might work with revolutionary effect. Most of our birds are helpless and generally resigned victims to the cow-bird, but there are indications of occasional effective protest among them. Thus the little Maryland yellow-throat, according to various authorities, often ousts the intruded egg, and its broken remains are also occasionally seen on the ground beneath the nests of the cat-bird and the oriole. The red-eyed vireo, on the other hand, though having apparently an easier task than the latter, in the lesser depth of her pensile nest, commonly abandons it altogether to the unwelcome speckled ovum—always, I believe, if the cow-bird has anticipated her own first egg.

But we have a more remarkable example of opposition in the resource of the little yellow warbler, which I have noted as one of the favorite dupes of the cow-bird—a deliberate, intelligent, courageous defiance and frequent victory which are unique in bird history, and which, if through evolutionary process they became the fashion in featherdom, would put the cow-bird's mischief greatly at a discount. The identity of this pretty little warbler is certainly familiar to most observant country dwellers, even if unknown by name, though its golden-yellow plumage faintly streaked with dusky brown upon the breast would naturally suggest its popular title of "summer yellow-bird." It is one of the commonest of the mnio-tiltidæ, or wood-warblers, though more properly a bird of the copse and shrubbery than of the woods. This nest is a beautiful piece of bird architecture. In a walk in search of one only a day or two ago I procured one, which is now before me. It was built in the fork of an elder-bush, to which it was moored by strips of fine bark and cobweb, its downy bulk being composed by a fitted mass of fine grass, willow cotton, fern wood, and other similar ingredients. It is about three inches in depth, outside measurement. But this depth greatly varies in different specimens. Our next specimen may afford quite a contrast, for the yellow warbler occasionally finds it to her interest to extend the elevation of her dwelling to a remarkable height. On page 50 is shown one of these nests, snugly moored in the fork of a scrub apple-tree. Its depth from the rim to the base, viewed from the outside, is about five inches, at least two inches longer than necessity would seem to require, and apparently with a great waste of material in the lower portion, as the hollow with the pretty spotted eggs is of only the ordinary depth of about two inches, thus hardly reaching half-way to the base. Let us examine it closely. There certainly is a suspicious line or division across its upper portion, about an inch below the rim, and extending more or less distinctly completely around the nest. By a very little persuasion with our finger-tip the division readily yields, and we discover the summit of the nest to be a mere rim—a top story, as it were—with a full-sized nest beneath it as a foundation. Has our warbler, then, come back to his last year's home and fitted it up anew for this summer's brood? Such would be a natural supposition, did we not see that the foundation is as fresh in material as the summit. Perhaps, then, the bird has already raised her first spring brood, and has simply extended her May domicile, and provided a new nursery for a second family. But either supposition is quickly dispelled as we further examine the nest; for in separating the upper compartment we have just caught a glimpse of what was, perhaps only yesterday, the hollow of a perfect nest; and, what is more to the point of my story, the hollow contains an egg—perhaps two, in which case they will be very dissimilar, one of delicate white with faint spots of brown on its larger end, the putting of the warbler, the other much larger, with its greenish surface entirely speckled with brown, and which, if we have had any experience in bird-nesting, we immediately recognize as the mischievous token of the cow-bird. We have discovered a most interesting curiosity for our natural-history cabinet—the embodiment of a presumably new form of intelligence in the divine plan looking to the survival of the fittest. It is not known how many years or centuries it has taken the little warbler to develop this clever resource to outwit the cow-bird. It is certain, however, that the little mother has got tired of being thus imposed upon, and is the first of her kind on record which has taken these peculiar measures for rising above her besetting trouble.

Who can tell what the future may develop in the nests of other birds whose homes are similarly invaded? I doubt not that this crying cow-bird and cuckoo evil comes up as a matter of consideration in bird councils. The two-storied nest may yet become the fashion in featherdom, in which case the cow-bird and European cuckoo would be forced to build nests of their own or perish.

But have we fully examined this nest of our yellow warbler? Even now the lower section seems more bulky than the normal nest should be. Can we not trace still another faint outline of a transverse division in the fabric, about an inch below the one already separated? Yes; it parts easily with a little disentangling of the fibres, and another spotted egg is seen within. A three-storied nest! A nest full of stories—certainly. I recently read of a specimen containing four stories, upon the top of which downy pile the little warbler sat like Patience on a monument, presumably smiling at the discomfiture of the outwitted cow-bird parasite, who had thus exhausted her powers of mischief for the season, and doubtless convinced herself of the folly of "putting all her eggs in one basket."

When we consider the life of the cow-bird, how suggestive is this spectacle which we may see every year in September in the chuckling flocks massing for their migration, occasionally fairly blackening the trees as with a mildew, each one the visible witness of a double or quadruple cold-blooded murder, each the grim substitute for a whole annihilated singing family of song-sparrow, warbler, or thrush! What a blessing, at least humanly speaking, could the epicurean population en route in the annual Southern passage of this dark throng only learn what a surpassing substitute they would prove—on toast—for the bobolinks which as "reed-birds" are sacrificed by the thousands to the delectable satisfaction of those "fine-mouthed and daintie wantons who set such store by their tooth"!

And what the cow-bird is, so is the Continental "cuckoo." Shall we not discriminate in our employment of the superlative? What of the throstle and the lark? Shall we still sing—all together:

DOOR-STEP NEIGHBOURS

ow little do we appreciate our opportunities for natural observation! Even under the most apparently discouraging and commonplace environment, what a neglected harvest! A back-yard city grass-plot, forsooth, what an invitation! Yet there is one interrogation to which the local naturalist is continually called to respond. If perchance he dwells in Connecticut, how repeatedly is he asked, "Don't you find your particular locality in Connecticut a specially rich field for natural observation?" The botanist of New Jersey or the ornithologist of Esopus-on-Hudson is expected to give an affirmative reply to similar questions concerning his chosen hunting-grounds, if, indeed, he does not avail himself of that happy aphorism with which Gilbert White was wont to instruct his questioners concerning the natural-history harvest of his beloved Selborne: "That locality is always richest which is most observed."

The arena of the events which I am about to describe and picture comprised a spot of almost bare earth less than one yard square, which lay at the base of the stone step to my studio door in the country.

The path leading to the studio lay through a tangle of tall grass and weeds, with occasional worn patches showing the bare earth. As it approached the door-step the surface of the ground was quite clean and baked in the sun, and barely supported a few scattered, struggling survivors of the sheep's-sorrel, silvery cinquefoil, ragweed, various grasses, and tiny rushes which rimmed the border. Sitting upon this threshold stone one morning in early summer, I permitted my eyes to scan the tiny patch of bare ground at my feet, and what I observed during a very few moments suggested the present article as a good piece of missionary work in the cause of nature, and a suggestive tribute to the glory of the commonplace. The episodes which I shall describe represent the chronicle of a single day—in truth, of but a few hours in that day—though the same events were seen in frequent repetition at intervals for months. Perhaps the most conspicuous objects—if, indeed, a hole can be considered an "object"—were those two ever-present features of every trodden path and bare spot of earth anywhere, ant-tunnels and that other circular burrow, about the size of a quill, usually associated, and which is also commonly attributed to the ants.

As I sat upon my stone step that morning, I counted seven of these smooth clean holes within close range, three of them hardly more than an inch apart. They penetrated beyond the vision, and were evidently very deep. Knowing from past experience the wary tenant which dwelt within them, I adjusted myself to a comfortable attitude, and remaining perfectly motionless, awaited developments. After a lapse of possibly five minutes, I suddenly discovered that I could count but five holes; and while recounting to make sure, moving my eyes as slowly as possible, my numeration was cut short at four. In another moment two more had disappeared, and the remaining two immediately followed in obscurity, until no vestige of a hole of any kind was to be seen. The ground appeared absolutely level and unbroken. Were it not for the circular depression, or "door-yard," around each hole, their location would, indeed, have been almost impossible. A slight motion of one of my feet at this juncture, however, and, presto! what a change! Seven black holes in an instant! And now another wait of five minutes, followed by the same hocus-pocus, and the black spots, one by one, vanishing from sight even as I looked upon them. But let us keep perfectly quiet this time and examine the suspected spots more carefully. Locating the position of the hole by the little circular "door-yard," we can now certainly distinguish a new feature, not before noted, at the centre of each—two sharp curved prongs, rising an eighth of an inch or more above the surface and widely extended.

What a danger signal to the creeping insect innocent in its neighborhood! How many a tragedy in the bug world has been enacted in these inviting, clean-swept little door-yards—these pitfalls, so artfully closed in order that their design may be the more surely effective. As I have said, these tunnels are commonly called "ant-holes," perhaps with some show of reason. It is true that ants occasionally are seen to go into them, but not by their own choice, while the most careful observer will wait in vain to see the ant come out again. Here at the edge of the grass we see one approaching now—a big red ant from yonder ant-hill. He creeps this way and that, and anon is seen trespassing in the precincts of the unhealthy court. He crosses its centre, when, click! and in an instant his place knows him no more, and a black hole marks the spot where he met his fate, which is now being duly celebrated in a supplementary fête several inches belowground.

A poor unfortunate green caterpillar, which, with a very little forcible persuasion in the interest of science, was induced to take a short-cut across this nice clean space of earth to the clover beyond, was the next martyr to my passion for original observation. He might have pursued his even course across the arena unharmed, but he too persisted in trespassing, and suddenly was seen to transform from a slow creeping laggard into the liveliest acrobat, as he stood on his head and apparently dived precipitately into the hole which suddenly appeared beneath him. A certain busy fly made itself promiscuous in the neighborhood, more than once to the demoralization of my necessary composure, as it crept persistently upon my nose. What was my delight when I observed the fickle insect in curious contemplation of a pair of calipers at the centre of one of the little courts! But, whether from past experience or innate philosophy in the insect I know not, the pronged hooks, though coming together with a click once or twice at the near proximity of the tempter, failed in their opportunity, and the trap was soon seen carefully set again, flush with the ground at the mouth of the burrow.

The contrast of these clean-swept door-yards with the mound of débris of the ants suggested an investigation of the comparative methods of burrowing and the disposal of the excavated material. Here is a hole evidently some inches in depth; what, then, has become of the earth removed? Suiting action to the thought, I swept into the openings of two or three of the holes quite a quantity of loose earth scraped from the close vicinity, and thus completely obliterated the opening of burrow, door-yard and all.

I awaited in vain any sign of returning activity at the surface, and, my patience being somewhat taxed, I entered my studio, where I remained for a quarter of an hour, perhaps. Upon stealing cautiously to the doorway, I observed all the obliterated holes had reappeared, and upon taking once more my original position I was soon rewarded with a demonstration of the method of excavation. After a moment or two a pellet of earth seemed suddenly to rise from within the cavity, and when arrived at the level of the ground was suddenly shot forth a distance of five or six inches, as though thrown from a tiny round flat shovel, which suddenly flashed from the opening, and as quickly retired to its depths, though not without a momentary display of two curved prongs and a formidable show of spider-like legs.

After a short lapse of time the act was repeated, this time a tiny stone being brought to the surface, and, after a brief pause at the doorway, was jerked to a distance as from a catapult. I now concluded to try the power of this propelling force, and taking a small stone, about three-quarters of an inch in length and a quarter-inch in thickness, laid it over the mouth of the tunnel. A few minutes passed, when I noticed a slight motion in the stone, immediately followed by a forcible ejectment, which threw it nearly an inch, the propelling instrument retiring so quickly into the burrow beneath as to scarce afford a glimpse. The stone appeared almost to have jumped voluntarily.

For an hour or more the bombardment of pellets and small stones continued from the mouth of the pit, until a small pile of the spent ammunition had accumulated at several inches distance, and at length the hole entirely disappeared, the earth in its vicinity presenting an apparently level surface—an armed peace, in truth, with the two touchy curved calipers on duty, as already described.

Following the hint of past experience, I concluded to explore the depths of one of these tunnels, especially as I desired a specimen of the wily tenant for portraiture; and it is, indeed, an odd fish that one may land on the surface if he be sufficiently alert in his angling. No hook or bait is required in this sort of fishing. Taking a long culm of timothy-grass, I inserted the tip into the burrow. It progressed without impediment two, three, six, eight inches, and when at the depth of about ten inches appeared to touch bottom, which in this kind of angling is the signal for a "strike" and the landing of the game. Instantly withdrawing the grass culm, I found my fish at its tip, from which he quickly dropped to the ground. His singular identity is shown in my illustration—an uncouth nondescript among grubs. His body is whitish and soft, with a huge hump on the lower back armed with two small hooks. His enormous head is now seen to be apparently circular in outline, and we readily see how perfectly it would fill the opening of the burrow like an operculum. But a close examination shows us that this operculum is really composed of two halves, on two separate segments of the body, the segment at the extremity only being the true head, armed with its powerful, sharp, curved jaws. As he lies there sprawling on his six spider-like legs, we may now easily test the skill of his trap, and gain some idea of his voracious personality.

If with the point of our knife-blade, holding it in the direction of the insect's body, we now touch its tail, what a display of vehement acrobatics! Instantly the agile body is bent backward in a loop, while the teeth fasten to the knife-blade with an audible click. If our finger-tip is substituted for the steel, the force of the stroke and the prick and grip of the jaws are unpleasantly perceptible.

In order to fully comprehend the make-up of this curious cave-dweller we must turn biologists for the moment. He must be considered from the evolutionary stand-point, or at least from the stand-point of comparative anatomy.

The first discovery that we make is that as we now see him he is crawling on his back—a fact which seems to have escaped his biographers heretofore. It is, in truth, the underside of his head which is uppermost at the mouth of the burrow, and his six zigzag legs are distorted backward to enable him to keep this contrary position. And what a hideous monster is this, whose flat, metallic, dirt-begrimed face stares skyward from this circular burrow! Well might it strike terror to the heart of the helpless insect which should suddenly find himself confronted by the motionless stare of these four cruel, glistening black eyes! But he is now a "fish out of water," and is about as helpless, nature never having intended him to be seen outside of his burrow—at least, in this present form. There he dwells, setting his circular trap at the mouth of his pitfall, and waiting for the voluntary sacrifice of his insect neighbors to fill his maw.

But this uncouth shape, which so courts obscurity, is not always thus so reasonably retiring. A few glass tumblers inverted above as many of these larger holes during the summer will intercept the winged sprite into which he is shortly to be transfigured—a brilliant metallic-hued beetle, perhaps flashing with bronzy gold or glittering like an emerald—the beautiful cicindela, or tiger-beetle, known to the entomologist as the most agile winged among the coleopterous tribe; known to the populace, perhaps, simply as a bright glittering fly that revels in the hot summer sands of the sea-shore or dusty country road, making its short spans of glittering flight from the very feet of the observer.

If we capture one of them with our butterfly-net he will be found to bear a general resemblance to the portrait here indicated—a slender-legged, proportionably large-headed beetle, with formidable jaws capable of wide extension, and re-enforced by an insatiate carnivorous hunger inherited from his former estate.

It will thus be seen that all the holes which we observe in the ground are not ant-holes; nor, indeed, are they monopolized by the tiger-beetles. There were other tunnels which I saw dug in my square yard of earth on that morning, which, while not of quite such depth, represented equally deep-laid plans.

While observing my cicindelas on that morning, my attention was at length diverted by an old friend of mine, who gave promise of much entertainment—a tiny black wasp, whose restless, rapid, zigzag, apparently aimless wanderings over the ground brought him into continual danger of contact with the snatching jaws of the cave-dwelling tiger, from which, however, he somehow escaped, though I distinctly heard the occasional clicking of the eager jaws.

With short abrupt flights or agile runs of a few inches, accompanied by nervous periodic flirts of the folded wings, the insect had covered pretty much of the ground in a short time, until she at length appeared to have discovered the object of her search, as she withdrew from beneath a sorrel leaf a big fat spider several times as large as herself. Its legs were folded beneath its body, and it was perfectly plain that this was not the first time that it had been in the toils of the wasp, which had evidently stung it into submission and stupor some minutes previous. Tugging bravely at her charge, the little black Amazon dragged her burden nimbly over the ground, pulling it after her in entire disregard of obstacles, now this way, now that, with the same exasperating disregard of eternity which she at first displayed, and at length deposited it on the top of a little flat weed, where it was left, while for five minutes more she pursued the same zigzag, apparently senseless meandering over the entire field of earth. Now she seems again to stumble upon her neglected prey, and taking it once more in her formidable jaws, she lugs it again for a long helter-skelter jaunt, this time depositing it in the neighborhood of a hole, which at first sight might have been considered an "ant-hole," from the débris which lay scattered about in its vicinity. After considerable needless delay, she is seen for once motionless, so far as her legs are concerned, but with her head over the tunnel, while, with flipping wings and rapidly waving antennæ, she investigates its depths. Satisfied that all is well, she again reaches her drowsy spider, by a tangled circuit of about a quarter of a mile—wasp measurement—and taking the victim in her teeth for the third time, finally succeeds in reaching the burrow, into which, without a particle of ceremony, she instantly retreats, dragging her helpless burden after her. Both wasp and spider are soon out of sight, and so remain perhaps for a space of two minutes, when the tips of the nervous antennæ appear at the doorway and the wasp emerges. What now follows is most curious and interesting. With an energy and directness in striking contrast to her previous proceedings, she proceeds to fill the cavity, biting the earth with her mandibles, and with her spiked legs kicking and shoving in the loose soil thus collected, ever and anon backing up to the hole and inserting the tip of her tail to force down the mass. As the filling is nearly completed, with the fore feet and jaws the surrounding earth is scraped for material, which she immediately proceeds to pack by a rhythmic tamping motion of the tail, until, at the end of five minutes, perhaps, the ground-level is finally reached, the surface smoothed, and no sign remains to mark the grave of the stupefied spider victim.

Not an hour after this episode I was treated to another of even more interest. As I took my seat upon the door-step I started into flight a big black wasp, upon whose doings I had evidently been intruding.

This wasp was much larger than the one just described, being about an inch in length. Its wings were pale brown and its body jet-black, with sundry small yellowish spots about the thorax. But its most conspicuous feature, and one which would ever fix the identity of the creature, was the long, slender, wire-like waist, occupying a quarter of the length of its entire body.

In a moment or two the wasp had returned, and stood at the mouth of the shallow pit. Eying me intently for a space, and satisfied that there was nothing to fear, she dived into the hollow and began to excavate, turning round and round as she gnawed the earth at the bottom, and shovelling it out with her spiked legs. Now and then she would back out of the burrow to reconnoitre, and her alert attitude at such times was very amusing—her antennæ drooping towards the burrow and in incessant motion; the abdomen on its long wire stem bobbing up and down at regular intervals, accompanied by a flipping motion of the wings; the short fore legs, one or both, upraised with comical effect.

As the tunnel was deepened a new method of excavation was employed. It has now reached a depth of an inch, only the extremity of the insect's body appearing, and the two hindermost legs clinging to surrounding earth for purchase. The deep digging is now accompanied by a continual buzzing noise, resembling that produced by a bluebottle fly held captive between one's fingers. At intervals of about ten or fifteen seconds the wasp would quickly back out of the burrow, bringing a load of sand, which it held between the back of the jaws and its thorax, sustained at the sides by the two upraised fore legs. After a moment's pause with this burden, the insect would make a sudden short darting flight of a foot or more in a quick circuit, hurling the sand a yard or more distant from the burrow. At the end of about fifteen minutes the burrow was sunk to the depth of an inch and a half, the wasp entirely disappearing, and indicated only by the continuous buzzing.

At this time, the luncheon hour having arrived, I was obliged to pause in my investigations, and in order to be able to locate the burrow in the event of its obliteration by the wasp before my return, I scratched a circle in the hard dirt, the hole being at its exact centre.

Upon my return, an hour later, I was met with a surprise. The ways of the digger-wasps of various species were familiar, but I now noted a feature of wasp-engineering which indeed seems to await its chronicler, as I find no mention of it by the wasp-historians.

At the exact centre of my circle, in place of a cavity, I now found a tiny pile of stones, supported upon a small stick and fragment of leaf, which had been first drawn across the opening.

This was evidently a mere temporary protection of the burrow, I reasoned, while the digger had departed in search of prey, and my surmise was soon proved to be correct, as I observed the wasp, with bobbing abdomen and flipping wings, zigzagging about the vicinity. Presently disappearing beneath a small plantain leaf, she quickly emerged, drawing behind her not a spider, as in the case of her smaller predecessor, but a big green caterpillar, nearly double her own length, and as large around as a slate-pencil—a peculiar, pungent, waspy-scented species of "puss-moth" larva, which is found on the elm, and with which I chanced to be familiar.

The victim being now ready for burial, the wasp sexton proceeded to open the tomb. Seizing one stone after another in her widely opened jaws, they were scattered right and left, when, with apparent ease and prompt despatch, the listless larva was drawn towards the burrow, into whose depths he soon disappeared. Then, after a short and suggestive interval, followed the emergence of the wasp, and the prompt filling in of the requisite earth to level the cavity, much as already described, after which the wasp took wing and disappeared, presumably bent upon a repetition of the performance elsewhere. But she had not simply buried this caterpillar victim, nor was the caterpillar dead, for these wasp cemeteries are, in truth, living tombs, whose apparently dead inmates are simply sleeping, narcotized by the venom of the wasp sting, and thus designed to afford fresh living food for the young wasp grub, into whose voracious care they are committed.

By inserting my knife-blade deep into the soil in the neighborhood of this burrow I readily unearthed the buried caterpillar, and disclosed the ominous egg of the wasp firmly imbedded in its body. The hungry larva which hatches from this egg soon reaches maturity upon the all-sufficient food thus stored, and before many weeks is transformed to the full-fledged, long-waisted wasp like its parent.

The disproportion in the sizes of the predatory wasps and their insect prey is indeed astonishing. The great sand-hornet selects for its most frequent victim the buzzing cicada, or harvest-fly, an insect much larger than itself, and which it carries off to its long sand tunnels by short flights from successive elevated points, such as the limbs of trees and summits of rocks, to which it repeatedly lugs its clumsy prey. In the present instance the contrast between the slight body of the wasp and the plump dimensions of the caterpillar was even more marked, and I determined to ascertain the proportionate weight of victor and victim. Constructing a tiny pair of balances with a dead grass stalk, thread, and two disks of paper, I weighed the wasp, using small square pieces of paper of equal size as my weights. I found that the wasp exactly balanced four of the pieces. Removing the wasp and substituting the caterpillar, I proceeded to add piece after piece of the paper squares until I had reached a total of twenty-eight, or seven times the number required by the wasp, before the scales balanced. Similar experiments with the tiny black wasp and its spider victim showed precisely the same proportion, and the ratio was once increased eight to one in the instance of another species of slender orange-and-black-bodied digger which I subsequently found tugging its caterpillar prey upon my door-step patch.

The peculiar feature of the piling of stones above the completed burrow was not a mere individual accomplishment of my wire-waisted wasp. On several occasions since I have observed the same manœuvre, which is doubtless the regular procedure with this and other species. The smaller orange-spotted wasp just alluded to indicated to me the location of her den by pausing suggestively in front of a tiny cairn. In this instance a small flat stone, considerably larger than the tunnel, had been laid over the opening, and the others piled upon it. On two occasions I have surprised this same species of wasp industriously engaged in the selection of a suitable flat foundation-stone with which to cover her burrow: her widely extended slender jaws enable her to grasp a pebble nearly a third of an inch in width.

In my opening vignette I have indicated two other door-step neighbors which bore my industrious wasps company in their arena of one square yard. To the left, surrounding a grass stem, will be seen an object which is unpleasantly familiar to most country folks—that salivary mass variously known by the libellous names of "snake-spit," "cow-spit," "cuckoo-spit," "toad-spit," and "sheep-spit," or the inelegant though expressive substitute of "gobs." The foam-bath pavilion of the "spume-bearer," with his glittering, bubbly domicile of suds, is certainly familiar to most of my readers; but comparatively few, I find, have cared to investigate the mysterious mass, or to learn the identity of the proprietor of the foamy lavatory.

The common name of "cow-spit," with the implied indignity to our "rural divinity," becomes singularly ludicrous when we observe not only the frequent generous display of the suds samples, thousands upon thousands in a single small meadow, but the further fact that each mass is so exactly landed upon the central stalk of grass or other plant—"spitted" through its centre, as it were. The true expectorator is within, laved in his own home-made suds. If we care to blow or scrape off the bubbles, we readily disclose him—— a green speckled bug, about a third of an inch in length in larger specimens, with prominent black eyes, and blunt, wedge-shaped body.

In the appended sketch I have indicated two views of him, back and profile, creeping upon a grass stalk. A glance at the insect tells the entomologist just where to place him, as he is plainly allied to the cicadæ, and thus belongs to the order Hemiptera, or family of "bugs," which implies, among other things, that the insect possesses a "beak for sucking." To what extent this tiny soaker is possessed of such a beak may be inferred from the amount of moisture with which he manages to inundate himself, which has all been withdrawn from the stem upon which he has fastened himself, and finally exuded from the pores of his body.

This is the spume-bearer, Aprophora, in his first or larval estate, which continues for a few weeks only. Erelong he will graduate from these ignominious surroundings, and we shall see quite another sort of creature— an agile, pretty atom, one of which I have indicated in flight, its upper wings being often brilliantly colored, and re-enforced by a pair of hind feet which emulate those of the flea in their powers of jumping, which agility has won the insect the popular name of "froghopper." They abound in the late summer meadow, and hundreds of them may be captured by a few sweeps of a butterfly-net among the grass.

My other remaining claimant for notice, shown upon the plant at the right margin of page 60, is a modest and inconspicuous individual, and might readily escape attention, save that a more intent observer might possibly wonder at the queer little tubular pinkish blossoms upon the plant—a rush—while a keen-eyed botanist would instantly challenge the right of a juncus to such a tubular blossom at all, especially at seed-time, and thus investigate. But the entomologist will probably classify this peculiar blossom at a glance, from its family resemblance to other specimens with which he is familiar. He will know, for instance, that this is a sort of peripatetic or nomadic blossom that will travel about on the plant, with which its open end will always remain in close contact. Many of the individuals are seen apparently growing upright out of the rounded seed-pod of the rush; and when the pink or speckled tube finally concludes to take up its travels, a clean round hole marks the spot of its tarrying, and an empty globular shell tells the secret of this brief attachment.

For this petal-like tube, so commonly to be seen upon the little rush of our paths, is, in truth, a tiny silken case enclosing the body of a small larva—a diminutive psychid, or sack-bearer, which I have not chanced to see described. Only the head and six prolegs of the occupant ever emerge from its case. Dragging its house along upon the plant, it attaches the open mouth of the sack close to the green seed-pod, after which the shell is gnawed through at the point of contact, and the young seeds devoured at pleasure, when a new journey is made to the next capsule, and thus until the maturity of the larva. At this time the case is about half an inch in length. It is now firmly attached to the plant. The opening is completely spun over with silk, and the case becomes a cocoon for the winter; and a few of these September cocoons are well worth gathering, if only to see the queer little moth which will emerge from them the following spring.

A QUEER LITTLE FAMILY ON THE BITTERSWEET

In a recent half-hour's relaxation, while comfortably stretched in my hammock upon the porch of my country studio, I was surprised with a singular entertainment. I soon found myself most studiously engaged. Entwining the corner post of the piazza, and extending for some distance along the eaves, a luxuriant vine of bittersweet had made itself at home. The currant-like clusters of green fruits, hanging in pendent clusters here and there, were now nearly mature, and were taking on their golden hue, and the long, free shoots of tender growth were reaching out for conquest on right and left in all manner of graceful curves and spirals. Through an opening in this shadowy foliage came a glimpse of the hill-side slope across the valley upon whose verge my studio is perched, and as my eye penetrated this pretty vista it was intercepted by what appeared to be a shadowed portion of a rose branch crossing the opening and mingling with the bittersweet stems. In my idle mood I had for some moments so accepted it without a thought, and would doubtless have left the spot with this impression had I not chanced to notice that this stem, so beset with conspicuous thorns, was not consistent in its foliage. My suspicions aroused, I suddenly realized that my thorny stem was in truth merely a bittersweet branch in masquerade, and that I had been "fooled" by a sly midget who had been an old-time acquaintance of my boyhood, but whom I had long neglected.

Every one knows the climbing-bittersweet, or "waxwork" (Celastrus scandens), with its bright berries hanging in clusters in the autumn copses, each yellow berry having now burst open in thin sections and exposed the scarlet-coated seeds. Almost any good-sized vine, if examined early in the months of July and August, will show us the thorns, and more sparingly until October, and queer thorns they are, indeed! Here an isolated one, there two or three together, or perhaps a dozen in a quaint family circle around the stem, their curved points all, no matter how far separated, inclined in the same direction, as thorns properly should be. Let us gently invade the little colony with our finger-tip. Touch one never so gently and it instantly disappears. Was ever thorn so deciduous? And now observe its fellows. Here one slowly glides up the stem; another in the opposite direction; another sideways. In a moment more the whole family have entirely disappeared, as if by hocus-pocus, until we discover, by a change of our point of view, that they have all congregated on the opposite side of the stem, with an agility which would have done credit to the proverbial gray squirrel.

Nor is this all the witchery of this bittersweet thorn. It is well worth our further careful study. Seen collectively, the thorny rose branch is instantly suggested, but occasionally, when we observe a single isolated specimen, especially in the month of July, he will certainly masquerade in an entirely new guise. Look! quick. Turn your magnifier hither on this green shoot. No thorn this. Is it not rather a whole covey of quail, mother and young creeping along the vine? Who would ever have thought of a thorn! Turning now to our original group, how perfectly do they take the hint, for are they not a family of tiny birds with long necks and swelling breasts and drooping tails, verily like an autumn brood of "Bob Whites"?

But the little harlequin is as wary a bird as he was a thorn! No sooner do we touch his head with our finger than with an audible "click" he is off on a most agile jump, which he extends with buzzing wings, and is even now perhaps aping a thorn among a little group of his fellows somewhere among the larger bittersweet branches.

It is only as we capture one of the little protean acrobats between our finger-tips and examine him with a magnifier that we can really make "head or tail" of his queer anatomy. Even thus enlarged it is difficult to get entirely rid of the idea of a bird. I have shown a group of the insects in various attitudes, the position of the eyes alone serving as a starting-point for our comprehension of his singular make-up. The tall neck-like or thorn-like prominence is then seen to be a mere elongated helmet, which is prolonged into a steep angle behind, so as to cover the back of the creature like a peaked roof, a feature from which the scientific name of this particular group of insects is derived, Membracis, meaning sharp-edged, the sides of the slope being covered by the close-fitting wings, which, though apparently compact with the body of the insect, are nevertheless always available for instant and most agile flight. We now discover two pairs of stout legs just beneath the edge of the wings, a third more slender pair being concealed behind, ready for immediate use in association with these buzzing wings when the whim of the midget prompts it to leap.

This insect is the tree-hopper, and is but one of many equally curious and

32

mimetic species to be found among the smaller branches of various trees and shrubs.

Our largest membracis is to be seen—with difficulty—on the terminal twigs of the locust-tree, its outlines so exactly imitating the thorny growths of the branch as to escape detection even by the closest scrutiny. Another remarkable species is a protégé of the oak, so closely simulating the warty bark of the smaller branches upon which it is found that our eyes may rest upon it repeatedly without recognizing it. The life history of these singular insects is quite similar, and is soon told. The membracis belongs to the tribe of "Bugs," Hemiptera, which implies that it possesses a beak instead of jaws, by which it sucks the sap of plants, precisely like the aphis, or plant-louse. This tiny beak we can readily distinguish bent beneath the body of our bittersweet hopper. Inserting it deep into the succulent bark, the parasite remains for hours as motionless as the thorn it imitates, the lower outline of its body hugging close against the bark. The curious suggestion of the thorn is produced not only by the outline, but by the curious fact that the hopper never sits across the twig, but always in the direction of its length; and, what is more, the projecting point of the thorax is always directed towards the end of the branch, or direction of growth. It is no easy thing even for the casual botanist to determine this nice point in a given segment of a bittersweet branch placed in his hand, the position of the chance leaf or leaf scar being his only guide. But the Membracis binotata rarely—indeed never, so far as I have examined—makes a mistake. Thus the wandering spray of bittersweet, recurve and twist upon itself as it may, will always disclose the little hopper or colony of them headed for its tip.

But I have omitted to mention one singular feature which is the usual accompaniment of my group of hoppers, and is, indeed, the most conspicuous sign of their presence on any given shrub. In the cut below I have indicated a short section of a bittersweet branch as it commonly appears, the twig apparently beset with tiny tufts of cotton, occasionally so numerous as to present a continuous white mass, usually on the lower side of the branch, where its direction is horizontal. They are thus easily seen from below, and a closer examination will always reveal one or more of the black animated thorns in their immediate vicinity, suggesting the responsible source. These tufts are pure white, a little over an eighth of an inch in length, and semicircular in vertical outline. The natural presumption is the idea of maternity, the mother hopper guarding her bundles of white eggs, or her infant hoppers, perhaps, snugly tucked up in their downy swaddling-clothes. But a closer examination completely dispels this illusion. Instead of the supposed fluffy cotton, we now discover the white substance to be of firm though somewhat sticky consistency, its surface, moreover, beautifully ridged from base to summit in parallel rounded flutings, which meet and interfold like a braid along the summit. If with a sharp knife we

33

now cut downward through and across the mass, we find our tuft to be a mere frothy shell containing two hollow compartments, with a thin central partition extending through the whole length of the cavity. But there is no sign of an egg or other life to be disclosed anywhere, either in its substance or its concealment. What, then, is the office of this tiny fragile house of congealed foam, with its snowy aerated structure, its double arched chambers, its corrugated walls and ceilings, and missing tenant or host? Such was the riddle which it propounded to me, and guided by some previous knowledge of the habits of allied insects, I was soon enabled to witness a solution of at least a part of its mystery.

This little thorn-like tree-hopper and all of its queer harlequin tribe are near relatives to the buzzing cicada, or harvest-fly, whose whizzing din in the dog-days has won it the popular misnomer of "locust."

To the average listener this insect is a mere "wandering voice and a mystery," and its singular form, wide prominent eyes, glassy wings, and double drums are always a surprise to the tyro who first identifies the grotesque as his well-known "locust." Its musical accomplishments during this brief period of its life are known to all, but few have cared to interest themselves in the early history of the singer, ere it perfected its musical resources "for the delight of man." But the naturalist, and especially the arboriculturist and fruit-grower, know to their cost of other tricks of the cicada, or rather of Mrs. Cicada, immortalized by Zenarchus the Rhodian as his "noiseless wife"—

I have alluded to the egg of the cicada "inserted in the bark of a twig." This act is accomplished by a knife-like ovipositor, which literally gouges a deep gash into the tender wood of various twigs, a number of the eggs being implanted in its depths, often causing the death of the branch. Shortly after hatching, the young cicadas leap for the ground, and burrowing beneath the surface, remain for a period varying from three to seventeen years, according to the species, to complete their transformations. Now the habits of my little tree-hopper are somewhat modelled after its big cousin. Knowing that the little insect was provided with a keen-edged ovipositor, and was in the habit of thrusting its tiny eggs beneath the bark, and realizing, too, that these strange tufts were of course in some way connected with the maternal instinct, I was led to investigate. Selecting a branch where the tufts and hoppers seemed most prolific, I brought my magnifying-glass to bear upon them at a respectful distance. Was ever actual thorn more motionless or non-committal than most of these?—their under surfaces hugging close against the bark, their telltale feet closely withdrawn, and all their pointed helmets inclined in the same parallel direction. One after another of the sly little family was examined without a revelation. Not until I had reached the upper limit of the group did I get any encouragement. Here I discovered one of the midgets in a new position, its

34

pointed helmet inclined farther downward, and its other extremity correspondingly raised, so that I could see beneath its body. I now observed what at first appeared to be the hind leg of the farther side of the body protruding beneath, but in another moment noted my error, and saw that its sharp point had penetrated the bark, into which it soon sank quite deeply, and I realized that the ovipositor was now conducting its tiny eggs into the cambium layer of the bark. Without waiting for this particular individual to finish her labors, which might be extended for hours for aught I knew, I turned my glass upon its nearest neighbor, and a most accommodating specimen she proved, disclosing all the mysteries of the little froth house, its strange material, and unique method of construction. What I saw reminded me irresistibly of the technique of the cake-frosting art of the fancy baker, with its flowing tube of white condiment, and its following tracery of questionable design in high relief. This accommodating specimen had apparently just completed her egg-laying, or had perhaps just filled one nest; and while her attitude was precisely similar to that of her neighbor, I noticed a tiny ball of glistening froth at the tip of the ovipositor. This was attached to the bark by a touch, and from this starting-point the construction of the glistening house was continued, the apex of the ovipositor pouring out its endless puffy roll of aerated cement, which seemed to set as soon as laid.

And what a convenient implement this for a froth-house builder who is compelled to work behind her back—mortar-feeder, trowel, darby, compass, and level all in one! Beginning with the first touch of the cement, the flowing point describes a very small half-circle to the right, again meeting the bark. It is now carried inward and upward, describing a very close circle with scarcely any space intervening, a similar circle being repeated on the left side. A new tier is then begun in the same manner, only this time a little larger in the sweep, and leaving a perceptible opening at the right as the central wall is carried upward with slightly decreased material. Returning down the central wall again, the white coil is carried to the left along the bark, and up again on the other outer edge, until it once more meets its fellow at the ridge-pole, where the two coils appear to interlock as in a braid. And thus the little builder continues, enlarging the cavity with each circuit, until the full height is reached, and then decreasing proportionately until the glistening braided dome is tapered off again against the bark.

Now what is the object of this frothy pavilion? The life history of the insect, in contrast to that of the cicada, will perhaps throw a little light on that question. In the cicada, as I have shown, the eggs are inserted in the bark, but the young, hatching about six weeks later, immediately forsake the parent tree and enter the ground. But the young of our bittersweet membracis are not thus fickle, the entire life of the insect being spent on the plant. Moreover, its eggs are laid in late summer, and do not hatch until the following spring. What, then, is this canopy of the tree-hopper but the provision of a thoughtful mother, a pavilion about her offspring as a shelter through the winter storms? In early July the tiny hoppers emerge from their egg-cases, and presumably creep out from their luminous domicile, and later on in the season these broods of varying numbers and all sizes are to be seen among the young stems of the plant, their beaks inserted, their pointed heads invariably in the same direction—towards the top of the branch. Even though in flight one of the midgets is seen to alight in violence to the rule, he instantly recognizes his mistake, and quickly glides round to the orthodox position.

This curious insect is chiefly confined to the bittersweet, though he is occasionally found in the company of a much bigger cousin of his on the branches of the locust, where these same telltale corrugated frothy pavilions are often seen to clothe the young twigs in their white tufts, the similar product of the larger species, which thus also presumably spends its entire life upon the locust-tree.

It is now some thirty years since the scientific world was startled by the publication of that wonderful volume, "The Fertilization of Orchids," by Charles Darwin; for though slightly anticipated by his previous work, "Origin of Species," this volume was the first important presentation of the theory of cross-fertilization in the vegetable kingdom, and is the one that is primarily associated with the subject in the popular mind. The interpretation and elucidation of the mysteries which had so long lain hidden within those strange flowers, whose eccentric forms had always excited the curiosity and awe alike of the botanical fraternity and the casual observer, came almost like a divine revelation to every thoughtful reader of his remarkable pages. Blossoms heretofore considered as mere caprices and grotesques were now shown to be eloquent of deep divine intention, their curious shapes a demonstrated expression of welcome and hospitality to certain insect counterparts upon whom their very perpetuation depended.

Thus primarily identified with the orchid, it was perhaps natural and excusable that popular prejudice should have associated the subject of cross-fertilization with the orchid alone; for it is even to-day apparently a surprise to the average mind that almost any casual wild flower will reveal a floral mechanism often quite as astonishing as those of the orchids described in Darwin's volume. Let us glance, for instance, at the row of stamens below (Fig. 1), selected at random from different flowers, with one exception wild flowers. Almost everybody knows that the function of the stamen is the secretion of pollen. This function, however, has really no reference whatever to the external form of the stamen. Why, then, this remarkable divergence? Here is an anther with its two cells connected lengthwise, and opening at the sides, perhaps balanced at the centre upon the top of its stalk or filament, or laterally attached and continuous with it; here is another opening by pores at the tip, and armed with two or four long horns; here is one with a feathery tail. In another the twin cells are globular and closely associated, while in its neighbor they are widely divergent. Another is club-shaped, and opens on either side by one or more upraised lids; and here is an example with its two very unequal cells separated by a long curved arm or connective, which is hinged at the tip of its filament; and the procession might be continued across two pages with equal variation.

As far back as botanical history avails us these forms have been the same, each true to its particular species of flower, each with an underlying purpose which has a distinct and often simple reference to its form; and yet, incredible as it now seems to us, the botanist of the past has been content with the simple technical description of the feature, without the slightest conception of its meaning, dismissing it, perhaps, with passing comment upon its "eccentricity" or "curious shape." Indeed, prior to Darwin's time it might be said that the flower was as a voice in the wilderness. In 1735, it is true, faint premonitions of its present message began to be heard through their first though faltering interpreter, Christian Conrad Sprengel, a German botanist and school-master, who upon one occasion, while looking into the chalice of the wild geranium, received an inspiration which led him to consecrate his life thence-forth to the solution of the floral hieroglyphics. Sprengel, it may be said, was the first to exalt the flower from the mere status of a botanical specimen.

This philosophic observer was far in advance of his age, and to his long and arduous researches—a basis built upon successively by Andrew Knight, Köhlreuter, Herbert, Darwin, Lubbock, Müller, and others—we owe our present divination of the flowers.

In order to fully appreciate this present contrast, it is well to briefly trace the progress, step by step, from the consideration of the mere anatomical and physiological specimen of the earlier botanists to the conscious blossom of to-day, with its embodied hopes, aspirations, and welcome companionships.

Most of my readers are familiar with the general construction of a flower, but in order to insure such comprehension it is well, perhaps, to freshen our memory by reference to the accompanying diagram (Fig. 2) of an abstract flower, the various parts being indexed.

The calyx usually encloses the bud, and may be tubular, or composed of separate leaves or sepals, as in a rose. The corolla, or colored portion, may consist of several petals, as in the rose, or of a single one, as in the morning-glory. At the centre is the pistil, one or more, which forms the ultimate fruit. The pistil is divided into three parts, ovary, style, and stigma. Surrounding the pistil are the stamens, few or many, the anther at the extremity containing the powdery pollen.

Although these physiological features have been familiar to observers for thousands of years, the several functions involved were scarcely dreamed of until within a comparatively recent period.

In the writings of ancient Greeks and Romans we find suggestive references to sexes in flowers, but it was not until the close of the seventeenth century that the existence of sex was generally recognized.

In 1682 Nehemias Grew announced to the scientific world that it was necessary for the pollen of a flower to reach the stigma or summit of the pistil in order to insure the fruit. I have indicated his claim pictorially at A (Fig. 3), in the series of historical progression. So radical was this "theory" considered that it precipitated a lively discussion among the wiseheads, which was prolonged for fifty years, and only finally settled by Linnæus, who reaffirmed the facts declared by Grew, and verified them by such absolute proof that no further doubts could be entertained. The inference of these early authorities regarding this process of pollination is perfectly clear from their statements. The stamens in most flowers were seen to surround the pistil, "and of course the presumption was that they naturally shed the pollen upon the stigma," as illustrated at B in my series. The construction of most flowers certainly seemed designed to fulfil this end. But there were other considerations which had been ignored, and the existence of color, fragrance, honey, and insect association still continued to challenge the wisdom of the more philosophic seekers. How remarkable were some of those early speculations in regard to "honey," or, more properly, nectar! Patrick Blair, for instance, claimed that "honey absorbed the pollen," and thus fertilized the ovary. Pontidera thought that its office was to keep the ovary in a moist condition. Another botanist argued that it was "useless material thrown off in process of growth." Krunitz noted that "bee-visited meadows were most healthy," and his inference was that "honey was injurious to the flowers, and that bees were useful in carrying it off"! The great Linnæus confessed himself puzzled as to its function.

For a period of fifty years the progress of interpretation was completely arrested. The flowers remained without a champion until 1787, when Sprengel began his investigations, based upon the unsolved mysteries of color and markings of petals, fragrance, nectar, and visiting insects. The prevalent idea of the insect being a mere idle accessory to the flower found no favor with him. He chose to believe that some deep plan must lie beneath this universal association. At the inception of this conviction he chanced to observe in the flower of the wild geranium (G. sylvaticum) a fact which only an inspired vision could have detected—that the minute hairs at the base of the petal, while disclosing the nectar to insects, completely protected it from rain. Investigation showed the same conditions in many other flowers, and the inference he drew was further strengthened by the remarkable discovery of his "honey-guides" in a long list of blossoms, by which the various decorations of spots, rings, and converging veins upon the petals indicated the location of the nectar.

His labors were now concentrated on the work of interpretation, until at length his researches, covering a period of two or three years, were given to the world. In a volume bearing the following victorious title, "The Secrets of Nature in Forms and Fertilization of Flowers Discovered," he presented a vast chronicle of astonishing facts. The previous discoveries of Grew and Linnæus were right so far as they went—viz., "the pollen must reach the stigma"—but those learned authorities had missed the true secret of the process. In proof of which Sprengel showed that in a great many flowers, as I have shown at C (Fig. 3), this deposit of pollen is naturally impossible, owing to the relative position of the floral parts, and that the pollen could not reach the stigma except by artificial aid. He then announced his startling theory:

But Sprengel's seeming victory was doomed to be turned to defeat. The true "secret" was yet unrevealed in his pages. He had given a poser to Linnæus (C), yet his own work abounded with similar strange inconsistencies, which, while being scarcely admitted by himself, or ingeniously explained, were nevertheless fatal to the full recognition of his wonderful researches. For seventy years his book lay almost unnoticed.

"Let us not underrate the value of a fact; it will one day flower in a truth." The defects in Sprengel's work were, after all, not actual defects. The error lay simply in his interpretation of his carefully noted facts. As Hermann Müller has said, "Sprengel's investigations afford an example of how even work that is rich in acute observation and happy interpretation may remain inoperative if the idea at its foundation is defective." What, then, was the flaw in Sprengel's work? Simply that he had seen but half the "secret" which he claimed to have "discovered." Starting to prove that insects fertilize the flowers, his carefully observed facts only served to demonstrate in many cases the reverse—that insects could not fertilize flowers in the manner he had declared. He was met at every hand, for instance, by floral problems such as are shown at E and F, where the pollen and the stigma in the same flower matured at different periods; and even though he recognized and admitted that the pollen must in many cases be transferred from one flower to another, he failed to divine that such was actually the common vital plan involved. It may readily be imagined that his great work precipitated an intense and prolonged controversy, and incited emulous investigation by the botanists of his time. Though a few of the more advanced of his followers, among them Andrew Knight (1799), Köhlreuter (1811), Herbert (1837), Gärtner (1844), clearly recognized the principle and foreshadowed the later theory of cross-fertilization, it was not until the inspired insight of Darwin, as voiced in his "Origin of Species," contemplated these strange facts and inconsistencies of Sprengel that their full significance and actual value were discovered and demonstrated, and his remarkable book, forgotten for seventy years, at last appreciated for its true worth. Alas for the irony of fate! Under Darwin's interpretation the very "defects" which had rendered Sprengel's work a failure now became the absolute witness of a deeper truth which Sprengel had failed to discern. One more short step and he had reached the goal. But this last step was reserved for the later seer. He took the fatal double problem of Sprengel—as shown at E and F, to express the consummation pictorially—and by the simple drawing of a line, as it were, as indicated between G and H, instantly reconciled all the previous perplexities and inconsistencies, thus demonstrating the fundamental plan involved in floral construction to be not merely "insect fertilization," the fatal postulate assumed by Sprengel, but cross-fertilization—a fact which, singularly enough, the latter's own pages proved without his suspicion.

Thus we see the four successive steps in progressive knowledge, from Grew in 1682, Linnæus, 1735, Sprengel, 1787, to Darwin, 1857-1858, and realize with astonishment that it has taken over one hundred and seventy-five years for humanity to learn this apparently simple lesson, which for untold centuries has been noised abroad on the murmuring wings of every bee in the meadow, and demonstrated in almost every flower.

This infinite field now open before him, Darwin began his investigations, and the whole world knows his triumphs. He has been followed by a host of disciples, to whom his books have come as an inspiration and ennobling impulse. Hildebrand, Delpino, Axell, Lubbock, and, latest and perhaps most conspicuous, Hermann Müller, to whom the American reader is especially referred. "The Fertilization of Flowers," by this most scholarly and indefatigable chronicler, presents the most complete compendium and bibliography of the literature on the subject that have yet appeared. Even to the unscientific reader it will prove full of revelations of this awe-inspiring interassociation and interdependence of the flower and the insect.

Many years ago the grangers of Australia determined to introduce our red clover into that country, the plant not being native there. They imported American seed, and sowed it, with the result of a crop luxuriant in foliage and bloom, but not a seed for future sowing! Why? Because the American bumblebee had not been consulted in the transaction. The clover and the bee are inseparable counterparts, and the plant refuses to become reconciled to the separation. Upon the introduction and naturalization of the American bumblebee, however, the transported clover became reconciled to its new habitat, and now flourishes in fruition as well as bloom.

Botany and entomology must henceforth go hand-in-hand. The flower must be considered as an embodied welcome to an insect affinity, and all sorts of courtesies prevail among them in the reception of their invited guests. The banquet awaits, but various singular ceremonies are enjoined between the cup and the lip, the stamens doing the hospitalities in time-honored forms of etiquette. Flora exacts no arbitrary customs. Each flower is a law unto itself. And how expressive, novel, and eccentric are these social customs! The garden salvia, for instance, slaps the burly bumblebee upon the back and marks him for her own as he is ushered in to the feast. The mountain-laurel welcomes the twilight moth with an impulsive multiple embrace. The desmodium and genesta celebrate their hospitality with a joke, as it were, letting their threshold fall beneath the feet of the caller, and startling him with an explosion and a cloud of yellow powder, suggesting the day pyrotechnics of the Chinese. The prickly-pear cactus encloses its buzzing visitor in a golden bower, from which he must emerge at the roof as dusty as a miller. The barberry, in similar vein, lays mischievous hold of the tongue of its sipping bee, and I fancy, in his early acquaintance, before he has learned its ways, gives him more of a welcome than he had bargained for. The evening primrose, with outstretched filaments, hangs a golden necklace about the welcome murmuring noctuid, while the various orchids excel in the ingenuity of their salutations. Here is one which presents a pair of tiny clubs to the sphinx-moth at its threshold, gluing them to its bulging eyes. Another attaches similar tokens to the tongues of butterflies, while the cypripedium speeds its parting guest with a sticking-plaster smeared all over its back. And so we might continue almost indefinitely. From the stand-point of frivolous human etiquette we smile, perhaps, at customs apparently so whimsical and unusual, forgetting that such a smile may partake somewhat of irreverence. For what are they all but the divinely imposed conditions of interassociation? say, rather, interdependence, between the flower and the insect, which is its ordained companion, its faithful messenger, often its sole sponsor—the meadows murmuring with an intricate and eloquent system of intercommunings beside which the most inextricable tangle of metropolitan electrical currents is not a circumstance. What a storied fabric were this murmurous tangle woven day by day, could each one of these insect messengers, like the spider, leave its visible trail behind it!

As a rule, these blossom ceremonies are of the briefest description. Occasionally, however, as in the cypripedium and in certain of the arums, or "jack-in-the-pulpit," and aristolochias, the welcome becomes somewhat aggressive, the guest being forcibly detained awhile after tea, or, as in the case of our milkweed, occasionally entrapped for life.

From this companionable point of view let us now look again at the strange curved stamen of the sage. Why this peculiar formation of the long curved arm pivoted on its stalk? Considered in the abstract, it can have no possible meaning; but taken in association with the insect to which it is shaped, how perfect is its adaptation, how instantly intelligible it becomes! Every one is familiar with the sage of the country garden, its lavender flowers arranged in whorls in a long cluster at the tips of the stems. One of these flowers, a young one from the top of the cluster, is shown at A (Fig. 4), in section, the long thread-like pistil starting from the ovary, and curving upward beneath the arch of the flower, with its forked stigma barely protruding (B). There are two of the queer stamens, one on each side of the opening of the blossom, and situated as shown, their anthers concealed in the hood above, and only their lower extremity appears below, the minute growth near it being one of the rudiments of two former stamens which have become aborted. If we take a flower from the lower portion of the cluster (D), we find that the thread-like pistil has been elongated nearly a third of an inch, its forked stigma now hanging directly at the threshold of the flower. The object of this will be clearly demonstrated if we closely observe this bee upon the blossoms. He has now reached the top of the cluster among the younger blossoms. He creeps up the outstretched platform of the flower, and has barely thrust his head within its tube when down comes the pair of clappers on his back (C). Presently he backs out, bearing a generous dab of yellow pollen, which is further increased from each subsequent flower. He has now finished this cluster, and flies to the next, alighting as usual on the lowermost tier of bloom. In them the elongated stigma now hangs directly in his path, and comes in contact with the pollen on his back as the insect sips the nectar. Cross-fertilization is thus insured; and, moreover, cross-fertilization not only from a distinct flower, but from a separate cluster, or even a separate plant. For in these older stigmatic flowers the anther as it comes down upon his back is seen to be withered, having shed its pollen several days since, the supply of pollen on the bee's body being sufficient to fertilize all the stigmas in the cluster, until a new supply is obtained from the pollen-bearing blossoms above. And thus he continues his rounds.

The sage is a representative of the large botanical order known as the Mint family, the labiates, or gaping two-lipped flowers, the arched hood here answering to the upper lip, the spreading base forming the lower lip, which is usually designed as a convenient threshold for the insects while sipping the nectar deep within the tube. This mechanism of the sage is but one of many curious and various contrivances in the Mint family, all designed for the same end, the intercrossing of the flowers.

While each family of plants is apt to favor some particular general plan, the modifications in the various species seem almost without limit.

Let us now look at the Heath family. The family of the heath, cranberry, pyrola, Andromeda, and mountain-laurel—how do these blossoms welcome their insect friends? This group is particularly distinguished by the unusual exception in the form of its anthers, which open by pores at their tips, instead of the ordinary side fissures. Two or three forms of these anthers are shown in my row of stamens (Fig. 1).

Seen thus in their detached condition, how incomprehensible and grotesque do they appear! And yet, when viewed at home, in their bell-shaped corollas, their hospitable expression and greeting are seen to be quite as expressive and rational as those of the sage. Take the mountain-laurel, for instance; what a singular exhibition is this which we may observe on any twilight evening in the laurel copse, the dense clusters of pink-white bloom waited upon by soft-winged fluttering moths, and ever and anon celebrating its cordial spirit by a mimic display of pyrotechnics as the anthers hurl aloft their tiny showers of pollen!

Every one is familiar with the curious construction of this flower, with its ten radiating stamens, each with its anther snugly tucked away in a pouch at the rim of its saucer-shaped corolla. Thus they appear in the freshly opened flower, and thus will they remain and wither if the flower is brought indoors and placed in a vase upon our mantel. Why? Because the hope of the blossom's life is not fulfilled in these artificial conditions; its natural counterpart, the insect, has failed to respond to its summons.

Here a tiny moth hovers above the tempting chalice, and now settles upon it with eager tongue extended for the nectar at its centre. What an immediate and expressive welcome! No sooner has this little feathery body touched the filaments than the eager anthers are released from their pockets, and, springing inwards, clasp their little visitor, at the same time decorating him with their compliments of webby pollen (A, Fig. 5).

The nectary now drained of its sweets, the moth creeps or flutters to a second blossom, and its pollen-dusted body thus coming in contact with its stigma, cross-fertilization is accomplished. The pollen of the laurel differs from that of most of the Heath blooms, its grains being more or less adherent by a cobwebby connective which permeates the mass as indicated in my magnified representation (B, Fig. 5).

It is probable that an accessory cross-fertilization frequently results from a mass of the pollen falling directly upon the stigma of a neighboring blossom, or even upon its own stigma, but even in the latter case, as has been absolutely demonstrated as a general law by the experiments of Darwin, the pollen from a separate flower is almost invariably prepotent, and leads to the most perfect fruition, and thus to the survival of the fittest—the cross-fertilized. And, in any event, the insect is to be credited for the release of the tiny catapults by which the pollen is discharged. But the laurel may be considered as an exceptional example of the Heath family. Let us look at a more perfect type of the order to which it belongs, the globular blossom of the Andromeda (A. ligustrina).

Only a short walk from my studio door in the country I recently observed its singular reception to the tiny black-and-white banded bee, which seems to be its especial companion, none the less constant and forgiving in spite of a hospitality which, from the human stand-point, would certainly seem rather discouraging. Fancy a morning call upon your particular friend. You knock at the door, and are immediately greeted at the threshold with a quart of sulphur thrown into your face. Yet this is precisely the experience of this patient little insect, which manifests no disposition to retaliate with the concealed weapon which on much less provocation he is quick to employ. Here he comes, eager for the fray. He alights upon one of the tiny bells scarce half the size of his body. Creeping down beneath it, he inserts his tongue into the narrowed opening. Instantly a copious shower of dust is poured down upon his face and body. But he has been used to it all his life, and by heredity he knows that this is Andromeda's peculiar whim, and is content to humor it for the sweet recompense which she bestows. The nectar drained, the insect, as dusty as a miller, visits another flower, but before he enters must of necessity first pay his toll of pollen to the drooping stigma which barely protrudes beneath the blossom's throat, and the expectant seed-pod above welcomes the good tidings with visions of fruition.

And how beautiful is the minute mechanical adaptation by which this end is accomplished! This species of Andromeda is a shrub of about four feet in height, its blossoms being borne in close panicled clusters at the summit of the branches. The individual flower is hardly more than an eighth of an inch in diameter. From one of three blossoms I made the accompanying series of three sectional drawings (Fig. 6). The first shows the remarkable interior arrangement of the ten stamens surrounding the pistil. The second presents a sectional view of these stamens, showing their peculiar S-shaped filaments and ring of anthers—one of the latter being shown separate at the right, with its two pores and exposed pollen. The freshly opened blossom discloses the entire ring of anthers in perfect equilibrium, each with its two orifices closed by close contact with the style, thus retaining the pollen. It will readily be seen that an insect's tongue, as indicated by the needle, in probing between them in search for nectar, must needs dislocate one or more of the anthers, and thus release their dusty contents, while the position of the stigma below is such as to escape all contact.

In most flowers, with the exception of the orchids, the stamens and pollen are plainly visible; but who ever sees the anthers of the blue-flag? Surely none but the analytical botanist and the companion insect to whom it is so artfully adjusted and so demonstrative. This insect is likely to be either a bumblebee or a species of large fly. In apt illustration of Sprengel's theory of the "path-finder" or honey-guide, the insect does not alight at the centre of the flower, but upon one of the three large drooping sepals, whose veins, converging to the narrow trough above, indicate the path to the nectar. Closely overarching this portion is a long and narrow curved roof—one of three divisions to the style, each surmounting its veined sepals. Beneath this our visiting bee disappears, and a glance at my sectional drawing shows what happens. Concealed within, against the ridge-pole, as it were, the anther awaits his coming, and in his passage to and from the nectar below spreads its pollen over his head and back. Having backed out of this segment of the blossom (A, Fig. 7), he proceeds to the next; but the shelf-like stigma awaits him at the door, and scrapes off or rubs off a few grains of the pollen from his back (B). Thus he continues until the third segment is reached, from which he carries away a fresh load of pollen to another flower. It will be seen that only the outer side of this appendage is stigmatic, and that it is thus naturally impossible for the blue-flag to self-fertilize— only one instance of thousands in which the anther and stigma, though placed in the closest proximity, and apparently even in contact—seemingly with the design of self-fertilization—are actually more perfectly separated functionally than if in separate flowers, the insect alone consummating their affinity.

In some flowers this separation is effected, as I have shown, by their maturing at different periods; in others, as in the iris, by mere mechanical means; while in a long list of plants, as in the willow, poplar, hemp, oak, and nettle, the cross-fertilization is absolutely necessitated by the fact of the staminate and stigmatic flowers being either separated on the same stalk or on different plants, the pollen being carried by insects or the wind. We may see a pretty illustration of this in the little wild flower known as the devil's-bit (Chamælirium luteum,), whose long, white, tapering spire of feathery bloom may often be seen rising above the sedges in the swamp. Two years ago I chanced upon a little colony of four or five plants at the edge of a bog. The flowers, all of them, were mere petals and stamens (B, Fig. 8). I looked in vain for a single stigmatic plant or flower; but far across the swamp, a thousand feet distant, I at length discovered a single spire, composed entirely of pistillate flowers, as shown in A (Fig. 8), and my magnifying-glass clearly revealed the pollen upon their stigmas—doubtless a welcome message brought from the isolated affinity afar by some winged sponsor, to whom the peculiar fragrance of the flower offers a special attraction, and thus to whom the fortunes of the devil's-bit have been committed.

In some flowers this separation is effected, as I have shown, by their maturing at different periods; in others, as in the iris, by mere mechanical means; while in a long list of plants, as in the willow, poplar, hemp, oak, and nettle, the cross-fertilization is absolutely necessitated by the fact of the staminate and stigmatic flowers being either separated on the same stalk or on different plants, the pollen being carried by insects or the wind. We may see a pretty illustration of this in the little wild flower known as the devil's-bit (Chamælirium luteum,), whose long, white, tapering spire of feathery bloom may often be seen rising above the sedges in the swamp. Two years ago I chanced upon a little colony of four or five plants at the edge of a bog. The flowers, all of them, were mere petals and stamens (B, Fig. 8). I looked in vain for a single stigmatic plant or flower; but far across the swamp, a thousand feet distant, I at length discovered a single spire, composed entirely of pistillate flowers, as shown in A (Fig. 8), and my magnifying-glass clearly revealed the pollen upon their stigmas—doubtless a welcome message brought from the isolated affinity afar by some winged sponsor, to whom the peculiar fragrance of the flower offers a special attraction, and thus to whom the fortunes of the devil's-bit have been committed.

The presence of fragrance and honey in a diœcious flower may be accepted in the abstract as almost conclusive of an insect affinity, as in most flowers of this class, notably the beech, pine, dock, grasses, etc., the wind is the fertilizing agent, and there is absence alike of conspicuous color, fragrance, and nectar—attributes which refer alone to insects, or possibly humming-birds in certain species.

Look where we will among the blossoms, we find the same beautiful plan of intercommunion and reciprocity everywhere demonstrated. The means appear without limit in their evolved—rather, I should say, involved—ingenuity. Pluck the first flower that you meet in your stroll to-morrow, and it will tell you a new story.

Only a few days since, while out on a drive, I passed a luxuriant clump of the plant known as "horse-balm." I had known it all my life, and twenty years previously had made a careful analytical drawing of the mere botanical specimen. What could it say to me now in my more questioning mood? Its queer little yellow-fringed flowers hung in profusion from their spreading terminal racemes. I recalled their singular shape, and the two outstretched stamens protruding from their gaping corolla, and could distinctly see them as I sat in the carriage. I had never chanced to read of this flower in the literature of cross-fertilization, and murmuring, half aloud, "What pretty mystery is yours, my Collinsonia?" prepared to investigate.

What I observed is pictured severally at Fig. 9, the flowers being shown from above, showing the two spreading stamens and the decidedly exceptional unsymmetrical position of the long style extending to the side. A small nectar-seeking bumblebee had approached, and in alighting upon the fringed platform grasped the filaments for support, and thus clapped the pollen against his sides. Reasoning from analogy, it would of course be absolutely clear that this pollen has thus been deposited where it will come in contact with the stigma of another flower. So, of course, it proved. In the bee's continual visits to the several flowers he came at length to the younger blooms, where the forked stigmas were turned directly to the front, while the immature stamens were still curled up in the flower tubes. Even the unopened buds showed a number of species where the early matured stigma actually protruded through a tiny orifice in precisely the right position to strike the pollen-dusted body of the bee, as he forced his tongue through the tiny aperture.[A]

If their dainty mechanism excite our wonder, what shall be said of the revelations in the great order of the Compositæ, where each so-called flower, as in the dandelion, daisy, cone-flower, marigold, is really a dense cluster of minute flowers, each as perfect in its construction as in the examples already mentioned, each with its own peculiar plan designed to insure the transfer of its own pollen to the stigma of its neighbor, while excluding it from its own?

All summer long the cone-flower, Fig. 10 (Rudbeckia hirta), blooms in our fields, but how few of us imagine the strange processes which are being enacted in that purple cone! Let us examine it closely. If we pluck one of the blossom's heads and keep it in a vase over-night, we shall probably see on the following morning a tiny yellow ring of pollen encircling the outer edge of the cone. In this way only are we likely to see the ring in its perfection, as in a state of nature the wind and insects rarely permit it to remain.

If we now with a sharp knife make a vertical section, as shown at A (Fig. 3), we may observe the conical receptacle studded with its embryo seeds, each bearing a tiny tubular blossom. Three distinct forms of these flowers are to be seen. The lower and older ones are conspicuous by their double feathery tails, the next by their extended anthers bearing the pollen at their extremity, and above these again the buds in all stages of growth. These various states are indicated in Fig. 11.

As in all the Compositæ, the anthers are here united in a tube, the pollen being discharged within. At the base of this anther-tube rises the pistil, which gradually elongates, and like a piston forces out the pollen at the top. Small insects in creeping over the cone quickly dislodge it. In the next stage the anthers have withered, the flower-tube elongated, and the top of the two-parted pistil begins to protrude, and at length expands its tips, disclosing at the centre the stigmatic surface, which has until now been protected by close contact. (See section.)

A glance at Fig. 11 will reveal the plan involved. The ring of pollen is inevitably scattered to the stigmas of the neighboring flowers, and cross-fertilization continually insured. Similar contrivances are to be found in most of the Compositæ, through the same method being variously applied.

Perhaps even more remarkable than any of the foregoing, which are more or less automatic in their movements, is the truly astonishing and seemingly conscious mechanism displayed in the wild arum of Great Britain—the "lords and ladies" of the village lanes, the foreign counterpart of our well-known jack-in-the-pulpit, or Indian-turnip, with its purple-streaked canopy, and sleek "preacher" standing erect beneath it. A representation of this arum is shown in Fig. 12, and a cross section at A, properly indexed.

How confidently would the superficial—nay, even careful—examination of one of the old-time botanists have interpreted its structure: "How simple and perfect the structure! Observe how the anthers are placed so that pollen shall naturally fall directly on the stigmas and fertilize them!" Such would indeed appear to be intended, until it is actually discovered that the stigmas have withered when the pollen is shed—a device which, acting in association with the little ring of hairs, tells a strange story. It is not my fortune to have seen one of these singular blossoms, but from the description of the process of fertilization given in Hermann Müller's wonderful work, aided by a botanical illustration of the structure of the flower, I am readily enabled to picture the progressive stages of the mechanism.

In the first stage (B, Fig. 13) small flies with bodies dusted with pollen from a previous arum blossom (for insects, as a rule, remain faithful or partial to one species of flowers while it is in bloom) are entering the narrowed tube, easily passing through the drooping fringe of hairs. Nectar is secreted by the stigmas, and here the flies assemble, thus dusting them with pollen. Their appetite temporarily satisfied, the insects seek escape, but find their exit effectually barred by the intruding fringe of hairs (C). In this second stage the stigmas, having now been fertilized, have withered, at the same time exuding a fresh supply of nectar, which again attracts the flies, whereupon, as shown at D, the anthers open and discharge their pollen upon the insects. In the fourth stage (E), all the functions of the flower having now been fulfilled, the fringe of hairs withers, and the imprisoned pollen-laden flies are permitted to escape to another flower, where the beautiful scheme is again enacted.

In a paper of this kind it is of course possible only to hint at a few representative examples of floral mechanisms, but these would be indeed incomplete without a closing reference to that wonderful tribe of flowers with which the theory of cross-fertilization will ever be memorably associated. I have previously alluded to the absolute dependence of the red clover upon the bumblebee. This instance may be considered somewhat exceptional, though numerous parallel cases are known. Among ordinary flowers this intervention of the insect is largely a preferable intention, and though almost invariably fulfilled, a large proportion of flowers still retain, as a dernier ressort, the power of at least partial self-fertilization and perpetuity in the absence or neglect of their insect counterpart.

The numerous and conclusive demonstrations of Darwin, however, have proved that in the competition for existence such self-fertilized offspring quickly yield before the progeny of cross-fertilization.

But the distinctive feature of the orchids lies in the fact that this dependence on the insect is wellnigh universally absolute. Here are a great host of plants which are doomed to extinction if for any reason their insect sponsors should permanently neglect them. The principal botanical feature which differentiates the orchid from other plants lies in the construction of the floral organs, the pistil, stigma, and anthers here being united into a distinct part known as the column. The pollen is, moreover, peculiar, being collected into more or less compact masses, and variously concealed in the flower. Some of these are club-shaped, with a viscid extremity, others of the consistency of a sticking-plaster, and all are hidden from external view in pouches and pockets, from which they never emerge unless withdrawn on the body of an insect. The various devices by which this removal is insured are most astonishing and awe-inspiring. Nor is it necessary to go to the conservatory for a tropical specimen, as is commonly supposed. An orchid is an orchid wherever it grows, and our native list of some fifty species will afford examples of as strange mechanical adaptations as are to be found among Darwin's pages. Indeed, a few of our American species are there described. One example will suffice for present illustration—the sweet-pogonia or grass-pink of our sedgy swamps (Pogonia ophioglossoides). Its solitary rosy blossom, nodding on its slender stem above the sedges, is always a welcome episode to the sauntering botanist, and its perfume, suggesting ripe red raspberries, is unique in the wild bouquet. One of these flowers is shown in profile at Fig. 14, its various parts indexed. Concealed behind the petals is the column, elsewhere indicated from various points of view. Attracted by its color and fragrance, the insect seeks the flower; its outstretched fringy lip offers a cordial invitation at its threshold, and conducts its visitor directly to the sweets above. In his entrance, as seen at D (Fig. 15), the narrowed passage compresses his back against the underside of the column, forcing his head and back against the stigma. The effect of this inward pressure, as will be seen, only serves to force the anther more firmly within its pocket; but as the insect, having drained the nectar, now backs out, note the result. The lip of the anther catches upon the back, swings outward on its hinge, and deposits its sticky pollen all over the insect's back, returning to its original position after his departure. In another moment he is seen upon another blossom, as at D again, his pollen-laden back now coming in contact with the stigma, and the intention of the blossom is accomplished; for without this assistance from the insect the little lid remains close within its pocket, and the pollen is thus retained.

What startling disclosures are revealed to the inward eye within the hearts of all these strange orchidaceous flowers! Blossoms whose functions, through long eras of adaptation, have gradually shaped themselves to the forms of certain chosen insect sponsors; blossoms whose chalices are literally fashioned to bees or butterflies; blossoms whose slender, prolonged nectaries invite and reward the murmuring sphinx-moth alone, the floral throat closely embracing his head while it attaches its pollen masses to the bulging eyes, or perchance to the capillary tongue! And thus in endless modifications, evidences all of the same deep vital purpose.

Let us then content ourselves no longer with being mere "botanists"— historians of structural facts. The flowers are not mere comely or curious vegetable creations, with colors, odors, petals, stamens, and innumerable technical attributes. The wonted insight alike of scientist, philosopher, theologian, and dreamer is now repudiated in the new revelation. Beauty is not "its own excuse for being," nor was fragrance ever "wasted on the desert air." The seer has at last heard and interpreted the voice in the wilderness. The flower is no longer a simple passive victim in the busy bee's sweet pillage, but rather a conscious being, with hopes, aspirations, and companionships. The insect is its counterpart. Its fragrance is but a perfumed whisper of welcome, its color is as the wooing blush and rosy lip, its portals are decked for his coming, and its sweet hospitalities humored to his tarrying; and as it finally speeds its parting affinity rests content that its life's consummation has been fulfilled.

A HONEY DEW PICNIC

Several of our notable as well as notorious human, social, and civic customs find their prehistoric prototypes in the insect kingdom. The monarchical institution sees its singular prophecy in the domestic economy of the bees. War and slavery have always been carried on systematically and effectually by ants, and, according to Huber and other authorities, agriculture, gardening, and an industry very like dairy farming have been time-honored customs among this same wise and thrifty insect tribe, whose claims to thoughtful consideration were so long ago voiced by Solomon of proverbial fame. Thévenot mentions "Solomon's ant" as among the "beasts which shall enter paradise." Indeed, the human saint as well as sluggard may "go to the ant" for many suggestive hints and commentaries.

These are only a few of the more notable parallelisms which suggest themselves. But others are not wanting if we care to follow the subject. In addition to the many models of thrift and virtuous industry, embodying types of many of the trade employments known to humanity, have we not also among these "meadow tribes" our luxurious "idlers" and "exquisites," the butterflies and flower-haunting flies and "dandy" beetles; and, opposed to all these, the suggestive antithesis of the promiscuous marauders, thieves, and brigands everywhere interspersed?

Thus we have our individual insect assassin and assassination organized in war; so, on the other hand, have we our insect merrymakers; why not, then, our picnic or carnival?

Such I am moved to call the singular episode which I observed last summer, and which I have endeavored to picture as true to the life as possible in the accompanying presentment The sceptic will perhaps remark on examination that the scene is characterized by somewhat too free a license to warrant the ideal of a "picnic." But he is hypercritical. There are

51

picnics and picnics—picnics of high and of low degree. Do I not recall more than one notorious festive outing of the "next lower than the angels" in which the personnel seemed about similarly proportioned, and the fun and attraction comparatively related to the license?

One July afternoon a year ago I was returning home from one of my botanizing strolls. I had just emerged from a deep wood, and was skirting its border, when my attention was caught by a small fluttering swarm of butterflies, which started up at my approach and hovered about a blossoming blackberry bush a few yards in advance of me at the side of my path. The diversity of the butterfly species in the swarm struck me as singular, and the mere allurement of the blackberry blossoms—not usually of especial attraction to butterflies—could hardly explain so extensive a gathering. Here was the great yellow swallow-tail (Turnus), red admiral (Atlanta), small yellow butterfly (Philodice), white cabbage-butterfly, comma and semicolon, and numerous small fry, fluttering about me in evident protest against my intrusion. They showed no inclination to vacate the premises, so, in pursuance of one of the first articles of my saunterer's creed, I concluded to retreat softly a few paces and watch for developments. One by one the swarm sought their original haunt, settling on the bramble, and I now noticed that only in occasional instances did the insects seek the flowers, the attraction seeming to be confined to the leaves. I stole up softly for a nearer point of observation, and could now distinctly see the beautiful yellow and black open wings of the swallow-tail softly gliding or gently fluttering as it hung from the edge of a leaf, while it explored its surface with its uncoiled capillary tongue. Just beyond my Turnus, on another leaf, I now noted a new presence, the orange Aphrodite butterfly, silvery spotted, its nether wings being folded over its back, too much absorbed to have been startled by my first approach. Occasionally, without any cause which I could detect from my present position—certainly in no way connected with my presence—a small swarm of the butterflies would rise in a flutter above the bush, as though actuated by a common whim—a brief winged tangle in which a beautiful sprite of velvety black hovering in a globular halo, shot through with two white semicircular arcs, was always a momentary feature.

Carefully stealing through the tall grass, I now approached to within touching distance of the haunt, and was soon lost in mingled wonder, amusement, and surprise at the picnic now disclosed, the occasional butterfly swarm being now easily explained. From my first point of view only the top of the bramble spray was visible above the grass, and by far the most interesting portion of the exercises had been concealed from view. The butterflies, while naturally the most conspicuous element, were now seen to be in a small minority among the insect gathering, the bramble leaves being peopled with a most motley and democratic assemblage of insects. Class distinctions were apparently forgotten in the common enthusiasm; the plebeian bluebottle and blowfly now consorted with Aphrodite and sipped at the same drop. Many a leaf was begemmed with the blue bodies closely set side by side or in a close cluster. The meat-fly, house-fly, and horse-fly made themselves promiscuous in every portion of the spray, and what with the rainbow-eyed and ruby-eyed flies, black and silver-banded flower-flies, and other tiny, restless, iridescent atoms of the fly fraternity, the family of Musca was well represented at the feast.

Nor were these all the guests at the banquet—for banquet there certainly was, judging from the eager sipping and crowding everywhere upon the leaves, the flowers even yet, as I first noticed, seeming to have little attraction.

I have no direct means of knowing as to the social discrimination of the host as shown in the entertainment, for that invitations were issued the subsequent facts would show. But I have good reasons for believing, from the course of events, that the gathering included a number of questionable personages that were not counted upon.

Here, for instance, was an overwhelming contingent of the whole tough gang of wasps and hornets—brown wasps from under the eaves and fences; black hornets from the big paper nests; yellow-jackets from where you please; deep steel-blue wire-waisted wasps from the mud cells in the garret, to say nothing of an occasional longer-waisted digger-wasp, and a host of their allied lesser associates scattered around generously among the assemblage.

Every now and then a big darning-needle took a shimmering circuit about the bush, and doubtless knew what he was about; as did also what at first glimpse appeared to be a big bumblebee, which seemed to find attraction in the neighborhood, although he seldom alighted upon the leaves, preferring to sit upon a neighboring weed and watch his opportunities.

I have thus described a few of the more prominent guests or personages present at the feast. But I have reported little of their "goings on." Doubtless there were appropriate toasts and responses, or what in bug etiquette answered to this seemingly indispensable human fad, while as to that other festive social essential of after-dinner speeches, coupled in this case with most vigorous discussion, I am certain the air was blue with something of this sort, if the eloquent pantomime bore any significance. Here, for instance, is one isolated, but frequent, episode. A peaceable little group of plain bluebottle-flies, with but a single thought, are all sipping at the same drop in contentment. A brief respite, for now the tips of a pair of inquisitive antennæ appear from the under edge of the leaf upon which they are sipping, and gingerly explore the upper surface. They are quickly followed by the covetous almond-eyed gaze of a brown wasp, that now steals cautiously around to the upper surface, and appears wholly engrossed in licking the leaf. Nearer and nearer he sidles up to the group of flies, and now with deliberate purpose and open jaws makes a dash among them. But they are too quick for him, and are away in a glittering blue tangle, which finally concentrates itself upon a neighboring leaf, where the eager tippling is immediately resumed. The wasp now holds the fort, and seems in no mood to be trifled with. With head and fore feet upraised and open jaws he seems "spoiling for a fight," and ready to make war upon the first comer. But no, he is evidently expecting a friend that, I now observe, approaches him determinedly down the stem of the leaf. The new-comer, a brown wasp like himself, is now at close range, and in an instant more, without any visible courteous preliminaries, the two set upon each other with a common enthusiasm, and with jaws working and stings fencing the interlocked combatants fall to the ground for a finish. I presume the affair was carried to the fourteenth round without any undue interference.

Another and another of these friendly meetings between them and other wasps took place in the half-hour in which I watched the sport. There were lulls in hostilities, during which an atmosphere of perfect peace and harmony seemed to reign around my bramble-bush. The flies were motionless in their ecstasy, and the hornet element seemed by common consent to keep temporarily shady, and even the butterflies seemed to forget that they had wings. But not for long, for now with a shimmering glitter our darning-needle invades the scene, and retires to a convenient perch with a ruby-eyed fly in his teeth, while a swarm of very startled butterflies tells conspicuously of the demoralization which he has left in his path. Among the butterfly representatives I at length observed one individual which at first had escaped me, an exclusive white cabbage-butterfly which sipped quietly at his leaf in the shade, and seemed to take little interest in the disreputable actions of his associates. Nothing could move him or entice him away from his convivial employment. But, alas! his folly soon found him out, for, on happening to look again, I observed he had found a new acquaintance—a hornet that had evidently been long desirous of meeting him. One by one I saw my butterfly's dismembered wings fall to the grassy jungle below, while a big black wasp proceeded to enjoy the collected sweets which he had doubtless observed were being so carefully stored away there in the shady retreat.

And now my pretty black butterfly—no, it proved to be the little day-flying grape-vine-moth, the eight-spotted black Alypia—appeared from some unseen source, and spun his crapy white-streaked halo among the leaves, at length settling among a little company of flies. Softly behind him creeps a brown wasp (Polistes), with his mouth watering, while from the opposite quarter a steel-blue mud-wasp approaches, with apparently similar designs. Neither invader sees the other. Simultaneously, as though answering to a signal, the two make a dash at the moth; but he is too quick for them. In a twinkling he is off in his pretty halo again, while the two disappointed contestants have clinched, and with stings and jaws vigorously plying fall to the jungle below, and seek satisfaction in mortal combat.

Here is a pretty little yellow and black banded flower-fly, which is having a quiet little picnic all by himself on a bed of yarrow bloom close by. But a big black paper-hornet has suddenly seen an attraction hither also, and is soon creeping stealthily among the blossoms with a wild and hungry look. But the hornets seemed to waste their time on the flies. Seemingly confident in their less complicated wing machinery, the two-winged fly rarely sought escape until within very close range of his enemy, and his resources never seemed to disappoint him at the critical moment.

Among the insect assemblage was a large number of ants of all kinds and sizes, the common large black species being conspicuous. Here is one creeping and sipping along a grass stem. A small digger-wasp likes this grass stem too, but instead of exchanging courtesies on the subject, the wasp proceeds to bite the ant's head off without ceremony, and continues sipping at the stem as though decapitation were a mere casual incident in its daily walk.

On the same stem a big blowfly has alighted. Judging from appearances, he has had his fill of good things, and is now making his leisurely toilet in the peculiar fashion of his kind, rubbing down his back and wings with his hind legs, twisting his front feet into spirals, and ever and anon testing the strength of his elastic neck attachment as he threatens to pull his head from his body.

This worldly act has been progressing for some moments under the gaze of a big black digger-wasp, who now concludes to cut it short. When at close range with his prey, the fly suddenly discovers the unhealthy location which he occupies, and actually protruding his tongue by way of parting salute, he is off with a buzz. He has barely taken wing, however, when a still louder buzz is heard, while a great black bumblebee follows closely in his wake, until the sounds of both are lost in the distance. The hum of this bumblebee is a frequent musical feature of the entertainment, and many is the dance that is set to its minstrelsy, as the burly insect darts in among the merrymakers and is off to his perch near by. It is only as we steal away and observe him closely that we learn the secret of his occasional sorties. There on a clover blossom he sits—sipping honey? Oh no. It is honey-dew that he is enjoying, and second-hand at that, as he devours the satiated bluebottle-fly which is empaled on his black horny beak. For this is only a bumblebee in masquerade—a carnivorous fly, in truth, which, safe in its disguise of respectability, hovers in the flowery haunts of the innocents and, of course, reaps his reward.

And what is this? A yellow-jacket has found an ambrosial attraction here upon the bramble leaf. Meanwhile a great black and white paper-hornet has seen his opportunity, and is soon slyly approaching behind the sipper. That he has designs on that jacket and its contents is apparent. In a moment the onslaught is consummated, and in the struggle which ensues the black assailant relieves his victim—of his watch presumably, for he has captured the entire garment, which he soon rifles and discards with some show of satisfaction.

And so my carnival proceeds. So it began with the dawn; so it will continue till dusk; and through the night, with new revels, for aught I know, and will be prolonged for days or weeks.

Reflective reader, how often, as you have strolled through some nook in the suburban wood, have you paused in philosophic mood at the motley relics of good cheer which sophisticated the retreat, so pathetically eloquent of pristine joys to which you had been a stranger? Here in my present picnic is the suggestive parallel, for even though no such actual episodes as those I have described had been witnessed by me, an examination of the premises beneath my bramble were a sufficient commentary. These were the unimpeachable witnesses of the pleasures which I have pictured. Dismembered butterfly wings strewed the grassy jungle, among which were a fair sprinkling from that black and white halo already noted. Occasional dead wasps and detached members of wasp and hornet anatomy were frequent, while the blue glitter of the bodies of flies lit up a shadowy recess here and there, showing that Musca had not always so correctly gauged his comparative wing resources as my observation had indicated.

It was interesting to discover, too, down deep among the herbage, another suggestive fact in the presence of a shrewd spider that showed a keen eye to the main chance, and had spread his gossamer catch-all beneath the bramble. It was all grist into his mill, and no doubt his charnel-house at the base of his silken tunnel could have borne eloquent testimony alike to his wise sagacity and his epicurean luxury.

I have pictured my picnic, and the question naturally arises, what was it all about—what the occasion for this celebration? There was certainly no distinct visible cause for the social gathering upon this particular bramble-bush. There were a number of other bramble-bushes in the near neighborhood which, it would seem, should possess equal attractions, but which were ignored. In what respect did the one selected differ from the others?

This bramble had become the scene of my carnival simply because it chanced to be directly beneath an overhanging branch of pine some twenty feet above. Here dwelt mine host who had issued the invitations and spread the feast, the limb for about a foot space being surrounded by a colony of aphides, or plant-lice, from whose distilling pipes the rain of sweet honey-dew had fallen ceaselessly upon the leaves below. The flies, butterflies, and ants had been attracted, as always, by its sweets; the preoccupied convivial flies, in turn, were a tempting bait for the wasps and hornets, and my dragon-fly and mock bumblebee found a similar attraction in the neighborhood.

An examination of the trunk of the pine showed the inevitable double procession of ants, both up and down the tree, with the habitual interchange of comment; and could we but have obtained a closer glimpse of the pine branch above, we might certainly have observed the queer spectacle of the small army of ants interspersed everywhere among the swarm of aphides. Not in antagonism; indeed, quite the reverse; herders, in truth, jealously guarding their feeding flock, creeping among them with careful tread, caressing them with their antennæ while they sipped at the honeyed pipes everywhere upraised in most expressive and harmonious welcome.

This intimate and friendly association of the ants and aphides has been the subject of much interesting scientific investigation and surprising discovery. Huber and Lubbock have given to the world many startling facts, the significance of which may be gathered from the one statement that certain species of ants carry their devotion so far as literally to cultivate the aphides, carrying them bodily into their tunnels, where they are placed in underground pens, reared and fed and utilized in a manner which might well serve as a pattern for the modern dairy farm. Indeed, after all that we have already seen upon a single bramble-bush, would it be taking too much license with fact to add one more pictorial chronicle—an exhilarated and promiscuous group of butterflies, ants, hornets, wasps, and flies uniting in "a health to the jolly aphis"?

A FEW NATIVE ORCHIDS AND THEIR INSECT SPONSORS

In a previous article I discussed the general subject of the fertilization of flowers, briefly outlining the several historical and chronological steps which ultimately led to Darwin's triumphant revelation of the divine plan of "cross-fertilization" as the mystery which had so long been hidden beneath the forms and faces of the flowers.

In the same paper I presented many illustrative examples among our common wild flowers possessing marvellous evolved devices, mechanisms, and peculiarities of form by which this necessary cross-fertilization was assured.

Prior to Darwin's time the flower was a voice in the wilderness, heard only in faintest whispers, and by the few. But since his day they have bloomed with fresher color and more convincing perfume. Science brought us their message. Demoralizing as it certainly was to humanity's past ideals, philosophic, theologic, and poetic, it bore the spirit of absolute conviction, and must be heard.

What a contrast this winged botany of to-day to that of a hundred years ago! The flower now no longer the mere non-committal, structural, botanical specimen. No longer the example of mere arbitrary, independent creation, reverently and solely referred to the orthodox "delight of man." The blossom whose unhappy fate was bemoaned by the poet because, forsooth, it must needs "blush unseen," or "waste its sweetness on the desert air," is found alone in that musty hortus siccus of a blind and deluded past. From the status of mere arbitrary creation, however "beautiful," "curious," "eccentric," hitherto accepted alone on faith—"it is thus because it is created thus: what need to ask the reason why?"—it has become a part of our inspiring heritage, a reasonable, logical, comprehensible result, a manifestation of a beautiful divine scheme, and is thus an ever-present witness and prophet of divine care and supervision.

The flower of to-day! What an inspiration to our reverential study! What a new revelation is borne upon its perfume! Its forms and hues, what invitations to our devotion! This spot upon the petal; this peculiar quality of perfume or odor; this fringe within the throat; this curving stamen; this slender tube! What a catechism to one who knows that each and all represent an affinity to some insect, towards whose vital companionship the flower has been adapting itself through the ages, looking to its own more certain perpetuation!

The great Linnæus would doubtless have claimed to "know" the "orchid," which perhaps he named. Indeed, did he not "know" it to the core of its physical, if not of its physiological, being? But could he have solved the riddle of the orchid's persistent refusal to set a pod in the conservatory? Could he have divined why the orchid blossom continues in bloom for weeks and weeks in this artificial glazed tropic—perhaps weeks longer than its more fortunate fellows left behind in their native haunts—and then only to wither and perish without requital? Know the orchid?—without the faintest idea of the veritable divorce which its kidnapping had involved!

Thanks to the new dispensation, we may indeed claim a deeper sympathy with the flower than is implied in a mere recognition of its pretty face. We know that this orchid is but the half of itself, as it were; that its color, its form, however eccentric and incomprehensible, its twisted inverted position on its individual stalk-like ovary, its slender nectary, its carefully concealed pollen—all are anticipations of an insect complement, a long-tongued night-moth perhaps, with whose life its own is mysteriously linked through the sweet bond of perfume and nectar, and in the sole hope of posterity.

And the flower had been stolen from its haunt while its consort slept, and had awakened in a glazed prison—doubtless sufficiently comfortable, save for the absence of that one indispensable counterpart, towards whom we behold in the blossom's very being the embodied expression of welcome.

Blooming day after day in anticipation of his coming, and week after week still hoping against hope, we see the flower fade upon its stalk, and with what one might verily believe to be evidences of disconsolation, were it not that the ultra-scientist objects to such a sentimental assumption with regard to a flower, which is unfortunate enough to show no sign of nerves or gray matter in its composition. Who shall claim to know his orchid who knows not its insect sponsor?

To take one of our own wild species. Here is the Arethusa bulbosa of Linnæus, for instance. Its pollen must reach its stigma—so he supposed—in order for the flower to become fruitful. But this is clearly impossible, as the pollen never leaves its tightly closed box unless removed by outside aid, which aid must also be required to place it upon the stigma. This problem, which confronted him in practically every orchid he met, Linnæus, nor none of his contemporaries, nor indeed his followers for many years, ever solved.

Not until the time of Christian Conrad Sprengel (1735) did this and other similar riddles begin to be cleared up, that distinguished observer having been the first to discover in the honey-sipping insect the key to the omnipresent mystery. Many flowers, he discovered, were so constructed or so planned that their pollen could not reach their own stigmas, as previously believed. The insect, according to Sprengel, enjoyed the anomalous distinction of having been called in, in the emergency, to fulfil this apparent default in the plain intentions of nature, as shown in the flower. Attracted by the color and fragrance of the blossom, with their implied invitation to the assured feast of nectar, the insect visited the flower, and thus became dusted with the pollen, and in creeping or flying out from it conveyed the fecundating grains to the receptive stigma, which they could not otherwise reach. Such was Sprengel's belief, which he endeavored to substantiate in an exhaustive volume containing the result of his observations pursuant to this theory.

But Sprengel had divined but half the truth. The insect was necessary, it was true, but the Sprengel idea was concerned only with the individual flower, and the great botanist was soon perplexed and confounded by an opposing array of facts which completely destroyed the authority of his work—facts which showed conclusively that the insect could not thus convey the pollen as described, because the stigma in the flower was either not yet ready to receive it—perhaps tightly closed against it—or was past its receptive period, even decidedly withered.

This radical assumption of fertilization in the individual flower, which lay at the base of Sprengel's theory, thus so completely exposed as false, discredited his entire work. The good was condemned with the bad, and the noble volume was lost in comparative oblivion—only to be finally resurrected and its full value and significance revealed by the keen scientific insight of Darwin (1859). From the new stand-point of evolution through natural selection the facts in Sprengel's work took on a most important significance. Darwin now reaffirmed the Sprengel theory so far as the necessity of the insect was concerned, but showed that all those perplexing floral conditions which had disproved Sprengel's assumption, instead of having for their object the conveying of pollen to the stigma of the same flower, implied its transfer to the stigma of another, cross-fertilization being the evident design, or evolved and perpetuated advantage.

This solution was made logical and tenable only on the assumption that such evolved conditions, insuring cross-fertilization, were of distinct advantage to the flower in the competitive struggle for existence, and that all cross-fertilized flowers were thus the final result of natural selection.

The early ancestors of this flower were self-fertilized; a chance seedling at length, among other continual variations, showed the singular variation of ripening its stigma in advance of its pollen—or other condition insuring cross-fertilization—thus acquiring a strain of fresh vigor. The seedlings of this flower, coming now into competition with the existing weaker self-fertilized forms, by the increased vigor won in the struggle of their immediate surroundings, and inheriting the peculiarity of their parent, showed flowers possessing the same cross-fertilizing device. The seeds from these, again scattering, continued the unequal struggle in a larger and larger field and in increasing numbers, continually crowding out all their less vigorous competitors of the same species, at length to become entire masters of the field and the only representatives left to perpetuate the line of descent.

Thus we find in almost every flower we meet some astonishing development by which this cross-fertilization is effected, by which the transferrence of the pollen from one flower to the stigma of another is assured, largely through the agency of insects, frequently by the wind and water, occasionally by birds. In many cases this is assured by the pollen-bearing flowers and stigmatic flowers being entirely distinct, as in cucumbers and Indian-corn; perhaps on different plants, as in the palms and willows; again by the pollen maturing and disseminating before the stigma is mature, as already mentioned, and vice versa.

From these, the simplest forms, we pass on to more and more complicated conditions, anomalies of form and structure—devices, mechanisms, that are past belief did we not observe them in actuality with our own eyes, as well as the absolutely convincing demonstration of the intention embodied: exploding flowers, shooting flowers, flower-traps, stamen embraces, pollen showers, pollen plasters, pollen necklaces, and floral pyrotechnics—all demonstrations in the floral etiquette of welcome and au revoir to insects.

From the simplest and regular types of flowers, as in the buttercup, we pass on to more and more involved and unsymmetrical forms, as the columbine, monk's-hood, larkspur, aristolochia, and thus finally to the most highly specialized or involved forms of all, as seen in the orchid—the multifarious, multiversant orchid; the beautiful orchid; the ugly orchid; the fragrant orchid; the fetid orchid; the graceful, homely, grotesque, uncanny, mimetic, and, until the year 1859, the absolutely non-committal and inexplicable flower; the blossom which had waited through the ages for Darwin, its chosen interpreter, ere she yielded her secret to humanity.

And what is an orchid? How are we to know that this blossom which we plucked is an orchid? The average reader will exclaim, "Because it is an air-plant"—the essential requisite, it would seem, in the popular mind. Of over 3000 known species of orchids, it is true a great majority are air-plants, or epiphytes—growing upon trees and other plants, obtaining their sustenance from the air, and not truly parasitic; but of the fifty-odd native species of the northeastern United States, not one is of this character, all growing in the ground, like other plants. It is only by the botanical structure of the flowers that the orchid may be readily distinguished, the epiphytic character being of little significance botanically.

A brief glance at this structural peculiarity may properly precede our more elaborate consideration of a few species of these remarkable flowers.

The orchids are usually very irregular, and six-parted. The ovary is one-celled, and becomes a pod containing an enormous yield of minute, almost spore-like, seeds (Fig. 3) in some species, as in the vanilla pod, to the number of a million, and in one species of the maxillaria, as has been carefully computed, 1,750,000.

The pollen, unlike ordinary flowers, is gathered together in waxy masses of varying consistency, variously formed and disposed in the blossom, its grains being connected with elastic cobwebby threads, which occasionally permit the entire mass to be stretched to four or five times its length, and recover its original shape when released. This is noticeable specially in the O. spectabilis, later described. The grains thus united are readily disentangled from their mass when brought into contact with a viscid object, as, for instance, the stigma.

But the most significant botanical contrast and distinction is found in the union of the style and stamens in one organ, called the column (Fig. 2), the stigma and the pollen being thus disposed upon a single common stalk. The contrast to the ordinary flower will be readily appreciated by comparison of the accompanying diagrams (Fig. 1).

When, therefore, we find a blossom with the anthers or pollen receptacle united to a stalk upon which the stigma is also placed, we have an orchid.

The order is further remarkable, as Darwin first demonstrated in his wonderful volume "The Fertilization of Orchids," in that the entire group, with very few exceptions, are absolutely dependent upon insects for their perpetuation through seed. They possess no possible resource for self-fertilization in the neglect of these insect sponsors.

Many of our common wild flowers, as perfectly and effectually planned for cross-fertilization as the orchids, do retain the reserve power of final self-fertilization if unfertilized by foreign pollen.

But the orchid has lost such power, and in the progress of evolution has gradually adapted itself to the insect, often to a particular species of insect, its sole sponsor, which natural selection has again gradually modified in relation to the flower.

The above work by Darwin was mostly concerned with foreign species, generally under artificial cultivation, and so startling were the disclosures concerning these hitherto sphinx-like floral beings that a most extensive bibliography soon attested the widespread inspiration and interest awakened by its pages.

But it is by no means necessary to visit the tropics or the conservatory for examples of these wonders. Our own Asa Gray, one of Darwin's instant proselytes, was prompt to demonstrate that the commonest of our native American species might afford revelations quite as astonishing as those exotic species which Darwin had described.

During a period of many years the writer has devoted much study to our native species of orchids from this evolutionary stand-point of their cross-fertilization tendencies. Of the following examples, selected from his list, some are elaborations of previous descriptions of Gray and others, though pictorially and descriptively the result of direct original study from nature; others are from actual observation of the insects at work on the flowers; and others still, original demonstrations based upon analogy and the obvious intention of the floral construction, the action of the insect—its head or tongue—having been artificially imitated by pins, bristles, or other probe-like bodies.

How many an enthusiastic flower-hunter has plucked his fragrant bouquet of the beautiful Arethusa, in its sedgy haunt, without a suspicion of the beautiful secret which lay beneath its singular form! Indeed, how many a learned botanist, long perfectly familiar with its peculiarities of shape and structure, has been entirely content with this simple fact, nor cared to seek further for its interpretation! But

"All may have the flower now,
For all have got the seed."

With Darwin as our guide and the insect as our key—an open sesame—the hidden treasure is revealed. It is now quite possible, as Darwin demonstrated, to look upon a flower for the first time and from its structure foretell the method of its intended cross-fertilization; nay, more, possibly the kind, or even the species, of insect to which this cross-fertilization is intrusted.

Let us look at our Arethusa. The writer has never happened to observe an insect at work upon this flower, but the intention of its structure is so plain that by a mere examination we may safely prophesy not only what must happen when the insect seeks its nectar, but with equal assurance the kind of insect thus invited and expected. I have indicated a group of the orchids in their usual marshy haunt, and in Fig. 4, separately, a series of diagrams presents sections of the flower, natural size and duly indexed, which renders detailed description hardly necessary. The column is here quite elongated, forked at the tip, the space between the forks occupied by the anther, which is hinged to the upper division. This anther lid is closed tightly, with the sticky mass of pollen hidden behind it in the cavity. The stigma is on the external inner side of the lower division, and thus distinctly separated from the pollen. The "lip" is extended forward as a hospitable threshold to the insect. And to what insect might we assume this invitation of color, fragrance, nectar, and threshold to be extended?

Let us consider the flower simply as a device to insure its own cross-fertilization. The insect is welcomed; it must alight and sip the nectar; in departing it must bear away this pollen upon its body, and convey it to the next Arethusa blossom which it visits, and leave it upon its stigma. These are the conditions expressed; and how admirably they are fulfilled we may observe when we examine flower after flower of a group, and find their nectaries drained, their anther cells empty, and pollen upon all their stigmas. The nectar is here secreted in a well—not very deep—and the depth of this nectar from the entrance is of great significance among all the flowers, having distinct reference to the length of the tongue which is expected to sip it. In the Arethusa, it is true, the butterfly or moth might sip at the throat of the flower, but the long tongues of these insects might permit the nectary to be drained without bringing their bodies in contact with the stigma. Smaller insects might creep into the nectary and sip without the intended fulfilment. It is clear that to neither of such visitors is the welcome extended. What, then, are the conditions embodied? The insect must have a tongue of such a length that, when in the act of sipping, its head must pass beyond the anther well into the opening of the flower. Its body must be sufficiently large to come in contact with the anther. Such requisites are perfectly fulfilled by the humblebee, and we may well hazard the prophecy that the Bombus is the welcomed affinity of the flower.

The diagrams (Fig. 4) sufficiently illustrate the efficacy of the beautiful plan involved. At A the bee is seen sipping the nectar. His forward movement thus far to this point has only seemed to press the edge of the anther inward, and thus keep it even more effectually closed. As the bee retires (B), the backward motion opens the lid, and the sticky pollen is thus brought against the insect's back, where it adheres in a solid mass. He now flies to the next Arethusa blossom, enters it as before, and in retiring slides his back against the receptive viscid stigma, which retains a portion of the pollen, and thus effects the cross-fertilization (C). Professor Gray surmised that the pollen was withdrawn on the insect's head, and it might be so withdrawn, but in other allied orchids of the tribe Arethusæ, however, in which the structure is very similar, the pollen is deposited on the thorax, and such is probably the fact in this species. In either case cross-fertilization would be effected. Nothing else is possible in the flower, and whether it is Bombus or not that effects it, the method is sufficiently evident.

Having thus had one initiation into this most enticing realm of riddles, each successive orchid whose structure we examine from this stand-point becomes a most interesting, perhaps a fresh, problem, whose assumed solution may often be verified by studying the insect in its haunts. Darwin thus foretold the precise manner of the cross-fertilization of Habenaria mascula, and also the insect agent, simply by the structural prophecy of the flower itself.

Suppose, for example, an unknown orchid blossom to be placed in our hands. Its nectary tube is five inches in length, and as slender as a knitting-needle. The nectar is secreted far within its lip. The evolution of the long nectary implies an adaptation to an insect's tongue of equal length. What insect has a tongue five inches long, and sufficiently slender to probe this nectary? The sphinx-moth only. Hence we infer the sphinx-moth to be the insect complement to the blossom, and we may correctly infer, moreover, that the flower is thus a night-bloomer. Examination of the flower, with the form of this moth in mind, will show other adaptations to the insect's form in the position of pollen and stigma, looking to the flower's cross-fertilization. In some cases this is effected by the aid of the insect's tongue; in others, by its eyes.

In our own native orchids we have a remarkable example of the latter form in the Habenaria orbiculata, whose structure and mechanism have also been admirably described by Asa Gray.

All orchid-hunters know this most exceptional example of our local flora, and the thrill of delight experienced when one first encounters it in the mountain wilderness, its typical haunt, is an event to date from—its two great, glistening, fluted leaves, sometimes as large as a dinner-plate, spreading flat upon the mould, and surmounted by the slender leafless stalk, with its terminal loose raceme of greenish-white bloom.

A single blossom of the species is shown in Fig. 5, the parts indexed. The opening to the nectary is seen just below the stigmatic surface, the nectary itself being nearly two inches in length. The pollen is in two club-like bodies, each hidden within a fissured pouch on either side of the stigma, and coming to the surface at the base in their opposing sticky discs as shown. Many of the group Habenaria or Platanthera, to which this flower belongs, are similarly planned. But mark the peculiarly logical association of the parts here exhibited. The nectary implies a welcome to a tongue two inches long, and will reward none other. This clearly shuts out the bees, butterflies, and smaller moths. What insect, then, is here implied? The sphinx-moth again, one of the lesser of the group. A larger individual might sip the nectar, it is true, but its longer tongue would reach the base of the tube without effecting the slightest contact with the pollen, which is of course the desideratum here embodied, and which has reference to a tongue corresponding to the length of the nectary. There are many of these smaller sphinxes. Let us suppose one to be hovering at the blossom's throat. Its slender capillary tongue enters the opening. Ere it can reach the sweets the insect's head must be forced well into the throat of the blossom, where we now observe a most remarkable special provision, the space between the two pollen discs being exactly adjusted to the diameter of the insect's head. What follows this entrance of the moth is plainly pictured in the progressive series of illustrations (Fig. 6). A represents the insect sipping; the sticky discs are brought in contact with the moth's eyes, to which they adhere, and by which they are withdrawn from their pouches as the moth departs (B). At this time they are in the upright position shown at C, but in a few seconds bend determinedly downward and slightly towards each other to the position D. This change takes place as the moth is flitting from flower to flower. At E we see the moth with its tongue entering the nectary of a subsequent blossom. By the new position of the pollen clubs they are now forced directly against the stigma (E). This surface is viscid, and as the insect leaves the blossom retains the grains in contact (F), which in turn withdraw others from the mass by means of the cobwebby threads by which the pollen grains are continuously attached. At G we see the orchid after the moth's visit—the stigma covered with pollen, and the flower thus cross-fertilized.

In effecting the cross-fertilization of one of the younger flowers its eyes are again brought into contact with this second pair of discs, and these, with their pollen clubs, are in turn withdrawn, at length perhaps resulting in such a plastering of the insect's eyes as might seriously impair its vision, were it not fortunately of the compound sort.

In another allied example of the orchids—the Showy Orchid—we have, however, what would appear a clear adaptation to the head of a bee, though one which might also avail of the service of an occasional butterfly. A group of this beautiful species is shown in my illustration. A favored haunt is the dark damp woods, especially beneath hemlocks, and with its deep pink hood and pure white lip is quite showy enough to warrant its specific title, "spectabilis." An enlarged view of the blossom is seen in Fig. 7, and in Fig. 8 a still greater enlargement of the column.

I have seen many specimens with the pollen masses withdrawn, and others with their stigmas well covered with the grains. Though I have never seen an insect at work upon it in its haunt, the whole form of the opening of the flower would seem to imply a bee, particularly a bumblebee. If we insert the point of a lead-pencil into this opening, thus imitating the entrance of a bee, its bevelled surface comes in contact with the viscid discs by the rupture of a veil of membrane, which has hitherto protected them. The discs adhere to the pencil, and are withdrawn upon it (Fig. 9). At first in upright position, they soon assume the forward inclination, as previously described. The nectary is about the length of a bumblebee's tongue, and is, moreover, so amply expanded at the throat below the stigma as to comfortably admit its wedge-shaped head. The three progressive diagrams (Fig. 10) indicate the result in the event of such a visit.

The pollen discs are here very close together, and are protected within a membraneous cup, in which they sit as in a socket. As the insect inserts his head at the opening (A) it is brought against this tender membrane, which ruptures and exposes the viscid glands of the pollen masses, which become instantly attached to the face or head, perhaps the eyes, of the burly visitor. As the insect retreats from the flower, one or both of the pollinia are withdrawn, as at B. Then immediately follows a downward movement, which exactly anticipates the position of the stigma, and as the bee enters the next flower the pollen clubs are forced against it (C), as in the previous example.

In the case of a smaller bee visiting the flower, the insect would find it necessary to creep further into the opening, and thus might bring its thorax against the pollen-glands. In either case the change of position in the pollinia would insure the same result.

We have thus seen adaptation to the thorax, the eyes, and the face in the three examples given. And the entrance of the flower in each instance is so formed as to insure the proper angle of approach for the insect for the accomplishment of the desired result. This direct approach, so necessary in many orchids, is insured by various devices—by the position of the lip upon which the insect must alight; by the narrowed entrance of the throat of the flower in front of the nectary; by a fissure in the centre of the lip, by which the tongue is conducted, etc.

Many other species allied to the above possess similar devices, with slight variations; and there is still another group whose structure is distinctly adjusted to the tongues of insects—adaptations not merely of position of pollen masses, but even to the extent of a special modification in the entrance to the flower and the shape of the sticky gland, by which it may more securely adhere to that sipping member.

In the common pretty Purple-fringed Orchid, whose dense cylindrical spikes of plumy blossoms occasionally empurple whole marshes, we have an arrangement quite similar to the H. orbicularis just described, with the exception that the pollen-pouches are almost parallel, and not noticeably spread at the base (Fig. 11). In this case the eyes of sipping butterflies occasionally get their decoration of a tiny golden club, but more frequently their tongues.

If, however, the butterfly should approach directly in front of the flower, as in a larger blossom he would be most apt to do, he might sip the nectar indefinitely and withdraw his tongue without bringing it in contact with the viscid pollen discs. But in the dense crowding of the flowers, over which the insect flutters indiscriminately, the approach is oftenest made obliquely, and thus the tongue brushes the disc on the side approached, and the pollen mass is withdrawn. But an examination of this orchid affords no pronounced evidence of any specific intention. There is no unmistakable sign to demonstrate which approach is preferred or designed by the flower, and this dependence on the insect's tongue or eye would seem to be left to chance.

In another closely allied species, however, we have a distinct provision which insures the proper approach of the tongue—one of many similar devices by which the tongue is conducted directly to one or the other of the pollen discs.

This is the Ragged Orchid, a near relative of the foregoing, H. psycodes, but far less fortunate in its attributes of beauty, its long scattered spike of greenish-white flowers being so inconspicuous in its sedgy haunt as often to conceal the fact of its frequency. Its individual flower is shown enlarged at Fig. 12—the lip here cut with a lacerated fringe (H. lacera). The pollen-pouches approach slightly at the base, directly opposite the nectary, where the two viscid pollen-glands stand on guard. Now were the opening of the nectary at this point unimpeded, the same condition would exist as in the H. psycodes—the tongue might be inserted between the pollen discs and withdrawn without touching them. But here comes the remarkable and very exceptional provision to make this contact a certainty—a suggestive structural feature of this flower of which I am surprised to find no mention either in our botanies or in the literature of cross-fertilization, so far as I am familiar with its bibliography. Even Dr. Gray's description of the fertilization device of this species makes no mention of this singular and very important feature. The nectary here, instead of being freely open, as in other orchids described, is abruptly closed at the central portion by a firm protuberance or palate, which projects downward from the base of the stigma, and closely meets the lip below.

The throat of the nectary, thus centrally divided, presents two small lateral openings, each of which, from the line of approach through the much-narrowed entrance of the flower, is thus brought directly beneath the waiting disc upon the same side. The structure is easily understood from the two diagrams Figs. 12 and 13, both of which are indexed.

The viscid pollen-gland is here very peculiarly formed, elongated and pointed at each end, and it is not until we witness the act of its removal on the tongue of the butterfly that we can fully appreciate its significance.

I have often seen butterflies at work upon this orchid, and have observed their tongues generously decorated with the glands and remnants of the pollen masses.

The series of diagrams (Fig. 14) will, I think, fully demonstrate how this blossom utilizes the butterfly. At A we see the insect sipping, its tongue now in contact with the elongated disc, which adheres to and clasps it. The withdrawal of the tongue (B) removes the pollen from its pouch. At C it is seen entirely free and upright, from which position it quickly assumes the new attitude shown at D. As the tongue is now inserted into the subsequent blossom this pollen mass is thrust against the stigma (E), and a few of the pollen grains are thus withheld upon its viscid surface as the insect departs (F).

In this orchid we thus find a distinct adaptation to the tongue of a moth or butterfly.

Another similar device for assuring the necessary side approach is seen in H. flava (Fig. 15), a yellowish spiked species, more or less common in swamps and rich alluvial haunts.

Fig. 14. The Ragged Orchid (H. Lacera) and the Butterfly's Tongue. Cross-fertilization

Professor Wood remarks, botanically, "The tubercle (or palate) of the lip is a remarkable character." But he, too, has failed to note the equally remarkable palate of the ragged orchid, just described, both provisions having the same purpose, the insurance of an oblique approach to the nectary. In H. flava this "tubercle," instead of depending from the throat, grows upward from the lip, and, as we look at the flower directly from the front, completely hides the opening to the nectary, and an insect is compelled to insert its tongue on one side, which direction causes it to pass directly beneath the pollen disc, as in H. lacera, and with the same result.

Of all our native orchids, at least in the northeastern United States, the Cypripedium, or Moccasin-Flower, is perhaps the general favorite, and certainly the most widely known. This is readily accounted for not only by its frequency, but by its conspicuousness. The term "moccasin-flower" is applied more or less indiscriminately to all species. The flower is also known as the ladies'-slipper, more specifically Venus's-slipper—as warranted by its generic botanical title—from a fancied resemblance in the form of the inflated lip, which is characteristic of the genus. We may readily infer that the fair goddess was not consulted at the christening.

There are six native species of the cypripedium in this Eastern region, varying in shape and in color—shades of white, yellow, crimson, and pink. The mechanism of their cross-fertilization is the same in all, with only slight modifications.

The most common of the group, the C. acaule, most widely known as the moccasin-flower, whose large, nodding, pale crimson blooms we so irresistibly associate with the cool hemlock woods, will afford a good illustration.

The lip in all the cypripediums is more or less sac-like and inflated. In the present species, C. acaule, however, we see a unique variation, this portion of the flower being conspicuously bag-like, and cleft by a fissure down its entire anterior face. In Fig. 16 is shown a front view of the blossom, showing this fissure. The "column" (B) in the cypripedium is very distinctive, and from the front view is very non-committal. It is only as we see it in side section, or from beneath, that we fully comprehend the disposition of stigma and pollen. Upon the stalk of this column there appear from the front three lobes—two small ones at the sides, each of which hides an anther attached to its under face—the large terminal third lobe being in truth a barren rudiment of a former stamen, and which now overarches the stigma. The relative position of these parts may be seen in the under view.

The anthers in this genus, then, are two, instead of the previous single anther with its two pollen-cells. The pollen is also quite different in its character, being here in the form of a pasty mass, whose entire exposed surface, as the anther opens, is coated with a very viscid gluten.

With the several figures illustrating the cross-fertilization, the reader will readily anticipate any description of the process, and only a brief commentary will be required in my text.

I have repeatedly examined the flowers of C. acaule in their haunts, have observed groups wherein every flower still retained its pollen, others where one or both pollen masses had been withdrawn, and in several instances associated with them I have observed the inflated lip most outrageously bruised, torn, and battered, and occasionally perforated by a large hole. I had observed these facts in boyhood. The inference, of course, was that some insect had been guilty of the mutilation; but not until I read Darwin's description of the cross-fertilization of this species did I realize the full significance of these telltale evidences of the escape of the imprisoned insect. Since that time, many years ago, I have often sat long and patiently in the haunt of the cypripedium awaiting a natural demonstration of its cross-fertilization, but as yet no insect has rewarded my devotion.

At length, in hopelessness of reward by such means, I determined to see the process by more prosaic methods. Gathering a cluster of the freshly opened flowers, which still retained their pollen, I took them to my studio. I then captured a bumblebee, and forcibly persuaded him to enact the demonstration which I had so long waited for him peaceably to fulfil. Taking him by the wings, I pushed him into the fissure by which he is naturally supposed to enter without persuasion. He was soon within the sac, and the inflexed wings of the margin had closed above him, as shown in section, Fig. 17. He is now enclosed in a luminous prison, and his buzzing protests are audible and his vehemence visible from the outside of the sac. Let us suppose that he at length has become reconciled to his condition, and has determined to rationally fulfil the ideal of his environment, as he may perhaps have already done voluntarily before. The buzzing ceases, and our bee is now finding sweet solace for his incarceration in the copious nectar which he finds secreted among the fringy hairs in the upper narrowed portion of the flower, as shown at Fig. 18 A. Having satiated his appetite, he concludes to quit his close quarters. After a few moments of more vehement futile struggling and buzzing, he at length espies, through the passage above the nectary fringe, a gleaming light, as from two windows

71

(A). Towards these he now approaches. As he advances the passage becomes narrower and narrower, until at length his back is brought against the overhanging stigma (Fig. 18 B). So narrow is the pass at this point that the efforts of the bee are distinctly manifest from the outside in the distension of the part and the consequent slight change in the droop of the lip. In another moment he has passed this ordeal, and his head is seen protruding from the window-like opening (A) on one side of the column. But his struggles are not yet ended, for his egress is still slightly checked by the narrow dimensions of the opening, and also by the detention of the anther, which his thorax has now encountered. A strange etiquette this of the cypripedium, which speeds its parting guest with a sticky plaster smeared all over its back. As the insect works its way beneath the viscid contact, the anther is seen to be drawn outward upon its hinge, and its yellow contents are spread upon the insect's back (Fig. 18 C), verily like a plaster. Catching our bee before he has a chance to escape with his generous floral compliments, we unceremoniously introduce him into another cypripedium blossom, to which, if he were more obliging, he would naturally fly. He loses no time in profiting by his past experience, and is quickly creeping the gantlet, as it were, or braving the needle's eye of this narrow passage. His pollen-smeared thorax is soon crowding beneath the overhanging stigma again, whose forward-pointed papillæ scrape off a portion of it (Fig. 18 B), thus insuring the cross-fertilizing of the flower, the bee receiving a fresh effusion of cypripedium compliments piled upon the first as he says "good-bye." It is doubtful whether in his natural life he ever fully effaces the telltale effects of this demonstrative au revoir.

Such, with slight modifications, is the plan evolved by the whole cypripedium tribe. Darwin mentions bees as the implied fertilizers, and doubtless many of the smaller bees do effect cross-fertilization in the smaller species. But the more ample passage in acaule would suggest the medium-sized Bombus as better adapted—as the experiment herewith pictured from my own experience many times would seem to verify, while a honey-bee introduced into the flower failed to fulfil the demonstration, emerging at the little doorway above without a sign of the cordial parting token.

Occasionally I suppose a fool bumblebee is entrapped within the petal bower and fails to find the proper exit, or it may be—much less a fool—having run the gantlet once too often, decides to escape the ordeal; hence the occasional mutilated blossom already described.

One of the most beautiful of our orchids, though its claims to admiration in this instance are chiefly confined to the foliage, is the common "Rattlesnake-Plantain," its prostrate rosettes of exquisitely white reticulated leaves carpeting many a nook in the shadows of the hemlocks, its dense spikes of yellowish-white blossoms signalling their welcome to the bees, and fully compensating in interest what they may lack in other attractive attributes.

The single flower is shown enlarged in Fig. 19—A, a young blossom, with analyses B and C, the latter indexed; D, an older blossom, with similar analyses (E and F). Both sorts are to be found upon every spike of bloom, as the inflorescence begins at the base and proceeds upward. As we look into the more open flower we observe a dark-colored speck, which, by analysis, proves to be the lid of the anther. This portion is further shown enlarged in Fig. 20, A. If we gently lift it with a pin, we disclose the pollen masses in the cavity (B) thus opened (C, profile section), the two pairs united to a common viscid gland at the base, this gland again secreted behind a veil of moist membrane, as also shown at B. This membrane is, moreover, very sensitive to the touch. Below the flattened tip of the column, and at a sharp inward angle, is the stigma. In the freshly opened flower (Fig. 19, A) the column inclines forward, bringing the anther low down, and its base directly opposite the V-shaped orifice in the lip, which also is quite firmly closed beneath the equally converging upper hood of the blossom. The entrance is thus much narrowed. If we insert a pin in this V-shaped entrance it comes in contact with the sensitive membrane below the anther, and it is immediately ruptured, as shown at Fig. 20, D. The sticky gland is brought into immediate contact, and clasps the pin, which, now being withdrawn, brings away the pollen, as in E and F. Thus it is naturally removed on the tongue of its sipping bee.

The further demonstration will be better shown by profile sections (Fig. 21). Nectar is secreted in the hollow of the lip indicated, somewhat as in the cypripedium. If we now imitate with a probe the habit of the insect and the action of its tongue, we may witness a beautiful contrivance for cross-fertilization. We will suppose the bee to be working at the top of the spike. He thrusts his tongue into the narrow opening (G). The membrane protecting the pollen-gland, thus surely touched, ruptures as described, and the exposed gland attaches itself to the tongue, being withdrawn as at H, and located on the insect's tongue, as in F, Fig. 20. The bee leaves this flower cluster and flies to another, upon which it will usually begin operation at the bottom. The flower thus first encountered is an old bloom, as in Fig. 19, D. Its sepals are more spreading, the lip slightly lowered, and the column so changed as to present the plane of the stigma, before out of sight, in such a new position as to invariably receive the pollen. The tongue of a bee entering this flower conveys the pollen directly against the stigmatic surface (I), which retains its disentangled fecundating grains, as at J, and the flower's functional adaptations are fulfilled.

In the allied Spiranthes, or "Lady's-Tresses," a somewhat similar mechanism prevails, by which fertilization is largely effected by the changed position or angle of the stigma plane.

And thus we might proceed through all the orchid genera, each new device, though based upon one of the foregoing plans, affording its new surprise in its special modification in adaptation to its insect sponsor—all these various shapes, folds of petals, positions, colors, the size, length, and thickness of nectary, the relative positions of pollen and stigma, embodying an expression of welcome to the insect with which its life is so marvellously linked. Occasionally this astounding affinity is faithful to a single species of insect, which thus becomes the sole sponsor of the blossom, without whose association the orchid would become extinct. A remarkable instance of this special adaptation is seen in the great Angræcum orchid of Madagascar, described by Darwin; and inasmuch as this species glorifies Darwin's faith in the truth of his theory, and marks a notable victory in the long battle for its supremacy, it affords an inspiring theme for my closing paragraphs.

Among the host of sceptics—and were they not legion?—who met this evolutionary and revolutionary theory with incredulity, not to say ridicule or worse, was one who thus challenged its author shortly after the appearance of his "Fertilization of Orchids," addressing Darwin from Madagascar substantially as follows: "Upon your theory of evolution through natural selection all the various contrasting structural features of the orchids have direct reference to some insect which shall best cross-fertilize them. If an orchid has a nectary one inch long, an insect's tongue of equivalent length is implied; a nectary six inches in length likewise implies a tongue six inches long. What have you to say in regard to an orchid which flourishes here in Madagascar possessing a long nectary as slender as a knitting-needle and eleven inches in length? On your hypothesis there must be a moth with a tongue eleven inches long, or this nectary would never have been elaborated."

Darwin's reply was magnificent in its proof of the sublime conviction of the truth of his belief: "The existence of an orchid with a slender nectary eleven inches in length, and with nectar secreted at its tip, is a conclusive demonstration of the existence of a moth with a tongue eleven inches in length, even though no such moth is known."

Many of us remember the ridicule which was heaped upon him for this apparently blind adherence to an untenable theory. But victory complete and demoralizing to his opponents awaited this oracular utterance when later a disciple of Darwin, led by the same spirit of faith and conviction, visited Madagascar, and was soon able to affirm that he had caught the moth, a huge sphinx-moth, and that its tongue measured eleven inches in length.

Here we see the prophecy of the existence of an unknown moth, founded on the form of a blossom. At that time the moth had not been actually seen at work on the orchid, but who shall question for a moment that had the flower been visited in its twilight or moonlight haunt the murmur of humming wings about the blossom's throat would have attested the presence of the flower's affinity, for without the kiss of this identical moth the Angræcum must become extinct. No other moth can fulfil the conditions necessary to its perpetuation. The floral adaptation is such that the moth must force its large head far into the opening of the blossom in order to reach the sweets in the long nectary. In so doing the pollen becomes attached to the base of the tongue, and is withdrawn as the insect leaves the flower, and is thrust against the stigma in the next blossom visited. This was clearly demonstrated by Darwin in specimens sent to him, by means of a probe of the presumable length and diameter of the moth's tongue. Shorter-tongued moths would fail to remove the pollen, and also to reach the nectar, and would thus soon learn to realize that they were not welcome.

The Angræcum also affords in this long pendent nectary a most lucid illustration of the present workings of natural selection. The normal length of that nectary should be about eleven inches, but in fact this length varies considerably in the flowers of different plants, this tendency to variation in all organic life being an essential and amply demonstrated postulate of the entire theory of natural selection. Let us suppose a flower whose nectary chances to be only six inches in length. The moth visits this flower, but the tip of its tongue reaches the nectar long before it can bring its head into the opening of the tube. This being a vital condition, the moth fails to withdraw the pollen; and inasmuch as the pollen is usually deposited close to the head of the moth, this flower would receive no pollen upon its stigma. This particular blossom would thus be both barren and sterile. None of its pollen would be carried to other stigmas, nor would it set a seed to perpetuate by inheritance its shorter nectary.

Again, let us suppose the variation of an extra long nectary, and the writer recently saw a number of these orchids with nectaries thirteen inches in length. The moth comes, and now must needs insert its head to the utmost into the opening of the flower. This would insure its fertilization by the pollen on the insect's tongue; and even though the sipper failed to reach the nectar, the pollen would be withdrawn upon the tongue, to be carried to other flowers, which might thus be expected to inherit from the paternal side the tendency to the longer nectary. The tendency towards the perpetuation of the short nectary is therefore stopped, while that of the longer nectary is insured.

THE MILKWEED

The singular hospitality of our milkweed blossom is nowhere matched among Flora's minions, and would seem occasionally in need of supervision.

Just outside the door here at my country studio, almost in touch of its threshold, year after year there blooms a large clump of milkweed (Asclepias cornuta), and, what with the fragrance of its purple pompons and the murmurous music of its bees, its fortnight of bloom is not permitted to be forgotten for a moment. Only a moment ago a whiff of more than usual redolence from the open window at which I am sitting reminded me that the flowers were even now in the heyday of their prime, and the loud droning music betokened that the bees were making the most of their opportunities.

Yielding to the temptation, I was soon standing in the midst of the plants. The purple fragrant umbels of bloom hung close about me on all sides, each flower, with its five generous horns of plenty, drained over and over again by the eager sipping swarm.

But the July sun is one thing to a bee and quite another thing to me. I have lingered long enough, however, to witness again the beautiful reciprocity, and to realize anew, with awe and reverence, how divinely well the milkweed and the bee understand each other. After a brief search among the blossom clusters I return to my seclusion with a few interesting specimens, which may serve as a text here at my desk by the open window.

Two months hence an occasional silky messenger will float away from the glistening clouds about the open milkweed pods, but who ever thanks the bees of June for them? The flower is but a bright anticipation—an expression of hope in the being of the parent plant. It has but one mission. All its fragrance, all its nectar, all its beauty of form and hue are but means towards the consummation of the eternal edict of creation—"Increase and multiply." To that end we owe all the infinite forms, designs, tints, decorations, perfumes, mechanisms, and other seemingly inexplicable attributes. Its threshold must bear its own peculiar welcome to its insect, or perhaps to its humming-bird friend, or counterpart; its nectaries must both tempt and reward his coming, and its petals assist his comfortable tarrying.

Next to the floral orchids, the mechanism of our milkweed blossom is perhaps the most complex and remarkable, and illustrates as perfectly as any of the orchid examples given in Darwin's noble work the absolute divine intention of the dependence of a plant species upon the visits of an insect.

Our milkweed flower is a deeply planned contrivance to insure such an end. It fills the air with enticing fragrance. Its nectaries are stored with sweets, and I fancy each opening bud keenly alert with conscious solicitude for its affinity. Though many other flowers manage imperfectly to perpetuate their kind in the default of insect intervention, the milkweed, like most of the orchids, is helpless and incapable of such resource. Inclose this budded umbel in tarlatan gauze and it will bloom days after its fellow-blooms have fallen, anticipating its consummation, but no pods will be seen upon this cluster.

What a singular decree has Nature declared with reference to the milkweed! She says, in plainest terms, "Your pollen must be removed on the leg of an insect, preferably a bee, or your kind shall perish from the face of the earth." And what is the deep-laid plan by which this end is assured? My specimens here on the desk will disclose it all.

Here are two bees, a fly, and a beetle, each hanging dead by its legs from a flower, an extreme sacrificial penalty, which is singularly frequent, but which was certainly not exacted nor contemplated in the design of the flower. A careful search among almost any good-sized cluster of milkweeds will show us many such prisoners. As in all flowers, the pollen of the milkweed blossom must come in contact with its stigma before fruition is possible. In this peculiar family of plants, however, the pollen is distinct in character, and closely suggests the orchids in its consistency and disposition. The yellow powdery substance with which we are all familiar in ordinary flowers is here absent, the pollen being collected in two club-shaped or, more properly, spatula-shaped masses, linked in pairs at their slender prolonged tips, each of which terminates in a sticky disc-shaped appendage united in V-shape below. These pollen masses are concealed in pockets (B) around the cylindrical centre of the flower, the discs only being exposed at the surface, at five equidistant points around its rim, where they lie in wait for the first unwary foot that shall touch them. A glance at the two views of this central portion of the flower, as it appears through my magnifying-glass—the honey-horns and sepals having been removed—will,

I think, indicate its peculiar anatomy or mechanism. No stigma is to be seen in the flower, the stigmatic surface which is to receive the pollen being concealed within five compartments, each of which is protected by a raised tent-like covering, cleft along its entire apex by a fine fissure (A). Outside of each of these, and entirely separated from the stigma in the cavity, lie the pollen masses within their pockets, each pair uniting at the rim below in V-shape, the union at the lower limit of the fissure.

With this more intimate knowledge of the floral anatomy, let us now visit our milkweed-plant and observe closely.

A bee alights upon the flower—the object of its visit being, of course, the sweets located in the five horn-shaped nectaries. In order to reach this nectar the insect must hang to the bulky blossom. Instantly, and almost of necessity, it would seem, one or more of the feet are seen to enter the upper opening of the fissure, and during the insect's movements are drawn through to the base. The foot is thus conducted directly between the two viscid discs, which immediately cling closer than a brother, and as the foot is finally withdrawn, the pollen is pulled from its cell. The member now released seeks a fresh hold, and the same result follows, the leg almost inevitably entering the fissure, and this time drawing in the pollen directly against the sticky stigmatic surface within. The five honey-horns have now been drained, and as our bee leaves the flower he is plainly detained by this too hearty "shake" or "grip" of his host, and quite commonly must exert a slight struggle to free himself. As the foot is thus forcibly torn away, the pollen mass is commonly scraped entirely off and retained within the fissure, or perhaps parts at the stalk, leaving the terminal disc clinging on the insect's leg. Occasionally, when more than one leg is entangled, the dangling blossom is tossed and swayed for several seconds by the vigorous pulling and buzzing, and a number of these temporary captives upon a single milkweed-plant are always to be seen.

Not unfrequently the mechanism so well adapted exceeds its functions and proves a veritable trap, as indicated in my specimens. I have found three dead bees thus entrapped in a single umbel of blossoms, having been exhausted in their struggles for escape; and a search among the flowers at any time will show the frequency of this fatality, the victims including gnats, flies, crane-flies, bugs, wasps, beetles, and small butterflies. In every instance this prisoner is found dangling by one or more legs, with the feet firmly held in the grip of the fissure.

Almost any bee which we may catch at random upon a milkweed gives perfect evidence of his surroundings, its toes being decorated with the tiny yellow tags, each successive flower giving and taking, exchanging compliments, as it were, with his fellows. Ordinarily this fringe can hardly prove more than an embarrassment; but we may frequently discern an individual here and there which for some reason has received more than his share of the milkweed's compliments. His legs are conspicuously fringed with the yellow tags. He rests with a discouraged air upon a neighboring leaf, while honey, and even wings, are seemingly forgotten in his efforts to scrape off the cumbersome handicap.

An interesting incident, apropos of our embarrassed bee, was narrated to me by the late Alphonso Wood, the noted botanist. He had received by mail from California a small box containing a hundred or more dead bees, accompanied by a letter. The writer, an old bee-keeper, had experience, and desired enlightenment and advice. The letter stated that his bees were "dying by thousands from the attacks of a peculiar fungus." The ground around the hive was littered with the victims in all stages of helplessness, and the dead insects were found everywhere at greater distances scattered around his premises. It needed only a casual glance at the encumbered insects to see the nature of the malady. They were laden two or three pairs deep, as it were, with the pollen masses of a milkweed. The botanist wrote immediately to his anxious correspondent, informing him, and suggesting as a remedy the discovery and destruction of the mischievous plants, which must be thriving somewhere in his neighborhood. A subsequent letter conveyed the thanks of the bee-keeper, stating that the milkweeds—a whole field of them—had been found and destroyed, and the trouble had immediately ceased. I am not aware that Mr. Wood ever ascertained the particular species of milkweed in this case. It is not probable that our Eastern species need ever seriously threaten the apiary, though unquestionably large numbers of bees are annually destroyed by its excessive hospitality. I have repeatedly found honey-bees dead beneath the plants, and my cabinet shows a specimen of a large bumblebee which had succumbed to its pollen burden, its feet, and even the hairs upon its body, being fringed deep with the tiny clubs—one of the many specimens which I have discovered as the "grist in the mill" of that wise spider which usually spreads his catch-all beneath the milkweeds.

Allied to the milkweed is another plant, the dogbane (Apocynum), which has a similar trick of entrapping its insect friends. Its drooping, fragrant, bell-shaped white flowers and long slender pods will help to recall it. But its method of capture is somewhat similar to the milkweed. The anthers are divided by a V-shaped cavity, into which the insect's tongue is guided as it is withdrawn from the flower, and into which it often becomes so tightly wedged as to render escape impossible. I have found small moths dangling by the tongue, as seen in the illustration below.

FOOTNOTE

[A] In numerous instances observed since the above was written I have noted the larger bumblebees upon the blossom. These insects have a different method of approach, hanging beneath the flower, the anthers being clapped against their thorax at the juncture of the wings, instead of the abdomen, as in the smaller bee.

THE END

www.ingramcontent.com/pod-product-compliance
Lightning Source LLC
Chambersburg PA
CBHW070602290526
45790CB00002B/752